Rest in God's Word

A Daily Devotional
from Genesis to Revelation

Kelly Brooke

Kelly Brooke

ISBN: 9798678320414

Cover design by: Art Painter & Kelly Brooke
Library of Congress Control Number: 2018675309
Printed in the United States of America

Introduction

This uplifting devotional includes one verse, a few words of encouragement, and a prayer for each day of the year. It includes scripture from every book of the Bible in order, starting with Genesis in January and ending with Revelation in December.

If you want to know God more, hear what He is telling you, see what He is showing you, realize where He is leading you, and know and understand His will for you, then accept His invitation to an intimate relationship. He is waiting ever so patiently for you. You develop a close and personal relationship with your Father by spending time with Him. Read the Bible to learn about His loving and faithful character, know what His promises are, and understand His will for your life. Starting each day with a devotional encourages your spirit and gives you a sense of peace.

Kelly's prayer for her readers is as follows:

Dear Heavenly Father,

May each person who reads this devotional be uplifted! Motivate them to pursue and maintain an intimate relationship with You, Lord. Reveal exactly what they need to hear, see, and feel from You as they read. Use this devotional to remind them of Your promises that never fail. Show them Your profound love and deep compassion. Remind them that your unending grace and continuous forgiveness are extended to them in all times. In Jesus name I pray, amen.

January 1

God said, 'Let there be light!' and there was.
~Genesis 1:3

Our King is so powerful and impressive that things can come into existence simply by the sound of His voice saying so. There is nothing impossible for Him! Whatever you're going through, be still and believe He can perform a miracle. Diseases can be cured, physical pain healed, hearts mended, relationships restored, anxiety wiped away, and so much more with simply God declaring it. What He says will happen will happen!

It is not always instantaneous though. More often than not, we wait for a period, whether a few days or a few years. Even though your prayer isn't answered immediately, He is working. He is waiting for us to trust Him more so that our faith can grow.

Dear Lord,

I praise your mighty name! I believe in you. Father, have the Holy Spirit give me more faith so that I can confidently trust you every moment of every day.

January 2

God said to Abram, "Leave your country, your people, and your father's household and go to the land I will show you."
~Genesis 12:1

Sometimes we need to desert our comfortable home, cut certain people loose, decline job opportunities, or surrender our own desires so that we can experience the incredible place God has ready to entrust to us. The beautiful blessing is there, right around the corner, and sometimes right in front of you! The promise He gave you is available. The miracle is waiting to be performed. God is just calling us to action, and sometimes this action involves leaving what and who we know, and/or stepping out of our comfort zone.

Abram was instructed to leave everyone and everything he knew. The Lord said "Go to the land I will show you." God didn't give him specific details about the journey. He simply instructed him to go (obey).

This is often how God works in our lives – leaving out specifications and details. He will give the details when we do our part, which is to obey. The word obey is a verb meaning to comply with the command/request. You do not need all the information in order to obey. Because God is your mighty protector, you can obey Him without doubting or being afraid. Be courageous and simply do what He instructs you to do, whether you have some of the details, or none at all.

Dear Father,

Help me to move forward to the land you have for me without being afraid. Even though I may not have all the facts or details, I choose to trust you. Thank you for your continual, loving presence.

January 3.

You intended to harm me, but God intended it for good to accomplish what's now being done, the saving lives of many.
~Genesis 50:20

There will be people who deliberately hurt you and knock you down, but always remind yourself that God will use everything you go through, including suffering, for good.

The coworker who spreads rumors behind your back, the family member who lies about you, the "friends" who discourage you, and anyone else who is simply hateful or malicious may try to hurt your feelings, cause you pain, and/or destroy your success. Praise God that you do not have to worry. The Lord is for you and He can take anything meant for evil and transform it into good.

We must also think of the bigger picture. It isn't always about us. As this verse states, God is using a negative situation to save many lives. Sometimes we go through an emotional, physical, or spiritual battle so that others can see our response of turning to God and in turn, they reach out to Him as well.

Dear Lord,

Please change my mindset to be glad hardships come. I want a heavenly perspective, seeing trials, heartache, pain, and stressful times as opportunities! You are for me and work all things out for good. Thank you for this opportunity to trust you more. Thank you for this opportunity to strengthen me. Thank you for this opportunity for your glory and power to shine!

January 4

"I am who I am. This is what you will say to the Israelites: 'I am has sent me to you.'"
~Exodus 3:14

God never needs to explain who He is or defend himself. He is the Prince of Peace, Everlasting Father, Wonderful Counselor, and Almighty God.

"Am" is the singular present tense form of the word "be." This tells us God is always present and unchanging. He is the same yesterday, today, and forever. People will disappoint you. People will leave you. One's character may fluctuate depending on the situation or who he/she is around. Our heavenly Father's loving, faithful, and gracious character are consistent and unwavering.

Dear God,

I am so grateful that you do not change! I can fully depend on you at any time, in any situation, and in any place. Thank you for your steadfast love and stable faithfulness.

January 5

Stand firm and you'll see the deliverance the lord will bring you today. ~Exodus 14:3

Don't hesitate. Don't tremble or shake. Don't worry or be uneasy. Stand firm so you can see and know just how He will free you! To "stand firm," hold on tightly to Truth. Search the Bible like you would search for gold. Find scripture that brightens your mind, encourages your heart, and restores your hope.

Surrender your heart, mind, and soul to Him. Then, the Holy Spirit will help you endure and overcome the storm you're in or the hardship you're struggling with. Jesus will keep you grounded during difficult times, so reach out to Him for help.

Dear God,

When I am on the battlefield, help me to remember that You are with me. I will not be afraid. Instead, I will remember Your promises and move forward confidently. Thank you for protecting me and leading me to victory.

January 6

The lord will fight for you. You only need to be still.
~Exodus 14:14

Sometimes, God calls us act, and other times He calls us to be still.

If He is clearly calling you to obey, there is no need to think about it or seek other people for advice. If God tells you to do something, do it without questioning Him or yourself and without being nervous or fearful.

If He doesn't want you to take action, then <u>just rest while trusting Him.</u> It is quite difficult to rest during hard times, but God is ready and waiting for you to call on His name for help. Be still and quiet so you can hear His gentle whispers.

Dear Lord,

I thank you for this fight I'm in right now because I know that you have already won the victory. When you call me to be still, I ask that the Holy Spirit quiets my mind when all I want to do is plan and think, silences my voice when all I want to do is argue, and stops my feet when all I want to do is go. Father, help me to be still while you fight for me.

January 7

The lord is my strength and my song. He has become my salvation. He is my God, and I'll praise Him, my father's God, and I'll exalt him.
~Exodus 15:2

When you feel completely defeated, praise the Lord that you don't need to rely on your own powerless strength! The Almighty is your strength! Call out to Him when you are exhausted, weak, or discouraged. Your Savior will rescue you from anything.

You can praise the Lord even when you're feeling helpless because it's in your weakness that His greatness is magnified! He can and does perform signs and wonders during times of deficiency. To see and experience His presence, praise and exalt Him in the turbulence of life!

Dear Heavenly Father,

Thank you for sending Jesus to save my soul! Thank You for securing my future in eternity. You are my strength when I feel like I can't move on. You are my power when I feel powerless. You are my song when I can't speak. I praise your glorious name!

January 8

You shall not make for yourself an image in the form of anything in heaven or earth or in the waters below.
~Exodus 20:4

Our Lord is a jealous God. He commands us to only worship Him as our lord. An "idol" is an image or representation of a god used as an object of worship or anyone/anything that's greatly admired and revered.

We must be on guard against this sin because idols can form in our minds quickly. Even if we have good intentions, like loving our spouse or being very career driven, when our minds become fixated on that person or career, our focus drifts further and further from God and closer to that idol.

If you love to plan, be on guard because if you are so focused on planning and your "to do list," you can lose sight of God. Your hobby can also be worshipped more than your heavenly Father. Your favorite television show, sports team, actor/actress, or other form of entertainment can easily become something you idolize.

Dear God,

If I ever begin praising someone or something other than You, stop me in my tracks. You are my God and I will worship You alone. I invite the Holy Spirit to always remind me that everything I have comes from You. Father, You deserve ALL the glory, praise, and honor.

January 9

Don't take advantage of foreigners who live among you in your land. ~Leviticus 19:33

To take advantage is to make unfair demands on someone who cannot or will not resist, or exploiting something for one's own benefit. A foreigner of a land is a person who is not from that place. Many people see strangers in their land as opportunities to deceive and/or take advantage of them. This is not godly living. Just because someone is a stranger doesn't give you the right to take advantage of him/her.

This verse reminds us to love everyone, regardless of where they come from or what they look like. Remember the times when you felt out of place (attending a new school, starting a new job, being completely out of your comfort zone somewhere). You wouldn't want to be mistreated or taken advantage of.

Treat outsiders as though they're insiders. God's greatest command of all is for us to LOVE everyone.

Dear Jesus,

Help me to be more like you, loving those who are different from me. Guard my heart from selfishness. Saturate my soul so that I can reflect your character to not only those closest to me, but to newcomers and foreigners as well.

January 10

You must be careful to keep all of my decrees and regulations by putting them into practice. I am the lord.
~Leviticus 19:37

Studying the Bible diligently and attending church regularly are wonderful, but in order to receive the abundant life God has for you, put His word into practice. Words are meaningless without action. Focus on how God wants you to apply His Truth in your life.

Prayer is a form of action. Talk with God, pouring out your heart, expressing your concern, asking for help, and simply telling him what's on your mind. Worship is also putting His word into action, for the Lord says to worship your one true God. Sing loudly, praising His glorious name in both good and bad times. Read His instructions carefully and obey. Forgive others, even your enemies. Love everyone, regardless of who they are, where they come from, what they do, what they look like, etc. Serve others and give to those in need.

Dear Jesus,

I know that your instructions and commands are for my good. Help me to be receptive as I read Your Word so that I can hear what you're trying to tell me. Holy Spirit, help me to apply God's truths in my personal life and in the lives of those around me.

January 11

If you follow my decrees and are careful to obey my commands, I'll send you the seasonal rains.
~Leviticus 26:3

The outcome of obedience is blessings. God will send you exactly what you need, and more, during the season you're meant to receive it. Each season yields certain crops. God also sends specific blessings and people during the different seasons of our lives.

Notice He will send "seasonal rains," meaning it won't rain continuously. There will be times of dryness when you feel like you're in the middle of the desert and nothing is going your way. There will be rough patches that need smoothing. There will be times of pain, struggle, and defeat. Take heart because that is just a season, and a very purposeful season at that. During times without rain, God is strengthening your character, growing your faith, and/or drawing you closer to Him. He may also be using your seasonal dryness for a special purpose in someone else's life. Sometimes we find out why we went through the dry period, but we also must understand that we may never know until we are in heaven. It doesn't matter whether we know why we experience it or not. What matters is that we trust God is in control.

Dear Father,

Thank you for my dry season. I know that it is for my benefit. I will wait in hopeful expectation for the rain You will send. Even though it is difficult, I know in my heart that it's just a season, and your blessings and answers to my prayers always come at the perfect time, exactly when I need it. Thank you for being in full control.

January 12

They marched for three days after leaving the mountain of the Lord, with the Ark of the Lord's Covenant moving ahead of them to show them where to stop and rest.
~Numbers 10:33

Moses made sure to place the Ark in front because He knew that God would guide them exactly where to go. Too often we seek either our own knowledge or others' help when we need direction before seeking God.

Yes, He may certainly give you the wisdom to go in a direction, but how will you know where to go without consulting Him first? He may place people in your life to show you the way as well, but how will you know if God has appointed them to do so without seeking Him first? God always knows the route for you to take! Go to Him first.

Notice here that God also shows them where to "stop and rest." Not only will God guide you on the right path, but He will tell you when to stop so you can relax and recharge. It is in the resting period that you can hear His gentle whispers.

Dear God,

I will seek your guidance first so that you can direct me on the right path. Thank you for going before me, showing me the way. Help me to take things one step at a time, slowing down and resting when you say to. Thank you for giving me the rest my mind, body, and soul need.

January 13

I will speak only the message that the lord puts in my mouth.
~Numbers 23:12

Balaam was faithful to the Lord and obeyed Him by telling King Balak exactly what God instructed him to say. Likewise, if we receive a word from God, we are not to twist it, leave certain parts out, or add to it. Obeying God means doing exactly as He says, whether it makes sense to you or not.

You do not need to worry about anything or the outcome because the Master of all creation is in complete control. He knows what is best for you. Obey Him at all times, no matter what. It may be difficult, but the blessing will surely outweigh the struggle.

Dear Jesus,

Please quiet my mind and open my ears so I can hear the words you have for me. I want to be your vessel, sharing the gospel. Please give me courage to speak your Truth in love.

January 14

O Lord, you are the God who gives breath to all creatures.
Please appoint a new man as leader for the community.
~Numbers 27:16

Moses first credits God for being responsible for all creation.
Then he requests Him to send a new leader to guide the
people so that they wouldn't be without a shepherd.

We must also remember that first and foremost, God is our
Creator who gives us breath. Second, we should follow
Moses' example and pray for our leaders which include
people directly involved in our daily lives such as bosses at
work, the pastors at church, government officials and law
enforcement, and our president and national leaders. They
have immense responsibilities and undergo a great deal of
pressure. We should be continuously praying that the Lord
gives them wisdom to lead and strength to persevere.

Respect them and their position regardless of your personal
opinions. Whether you agree with how they lead and/or their
decisions is beside the point. God has chosen them to be in
charge at that specific time, so respect His decision. If they are
leading unfairly, negatively, or in a way that harms people,
still pray for them. God always has a purpose for His ways.
Remember, He tells us to love our enemies and pray for those
who persecute us.

Dear Lord,

Give the leaders of my country wisdom to make tough decisions and strength to persevere during epidemics, natural disasters, war, and other times of chaos. Guide my administrators and boss at work to be great, encouraging leaders. Fill their hearts with your peace and joy. You put them in charge right now for Your purposes. Help me demonstrate respect towards them even when I disagree with them because I want to always honor You.

January 15

If you obey all the decrees and commands I'm giving you today, all will be well with you and your children. I'm giving you these instructions so you'll enjoy a long life in the land the lord your God is giving you for all time.
~Deuteronomy 4:40

Note the words *if* and *all will be well*. Trust in the Lord and obey Him, for the outcome includes many blessings and longevity not only for you, but for your children, grandchildren, and generations to follow.

God has a beautiful land full of blessings for you! He wants you to go there and to enjoy it. You just need to do your part – obey His instructions.

Dear Jesus,

Thank you for all the blessings you've given me and for those yet to come. I know that obedience leads to blessings, so Father, keep me attuned to Your voice so that I can hear what You're telling me to do. My greatest desire is to do Your will.

January 16

Do what is right and good in the Lord's sight so all will go well with you. ~Deuteronomy 6:18

You cannot receive all that God has for you unless you live righteously. Read and mediate on the Bible to understand His character so that you can know what is good and pleasing to Him. When you put His word into practice by giving to those in need, serving others, and above all loving everyone, you will "enter and occupy the good land" God has ready for you. There isn't a free ticket. Show the Lord you love Him by doing what is good and pleasing to Him.

Dear God,

As I read your word, teach me what is good and pleasing to you. Point out to me what I need to change in my attitude, thoughts, and/or actions. I surrender to You so that You can work freely within me to make me a better person.

January 17

But you have seen the Lord perform all these mighty deeds with your own eyes! ~Deuteronomy 11:7

His miracles, signs, and wonders are present every day! Breathtaking sunsets and sunrises, stunning landforms, and amazing animals abound. People perform beautiful acts of kindness, give generously to the poor and homeless, and give up their own time and desires in order to serve others. A fatal disease is completely healed, a shattered relationship is restored, and an impossible situation suddenly is possible because God made a way.

There are people all around you – at the workplace, the grocery store, the mall – who have not seen the work of our divine Savior either because their eyes are too clouded, they don't believe in Him, or they simply don't know of Him.

So, share all the miracles, signs, and wonders you've seen with your family, friends, coworkers, and everyone, giving all the glory to God so they realize that the credit belongs to Him.

Dear Jesus,

Please keep my path of vision clear of all clutter and debris so that I can see all of your amazing wonders and incredible miracles. Drown out the noise of the world so that I can hear your whispers. Holy Spirit, give me the confidence to share the gospel and my testimony. I want to be your vessel, leading as many people to You as I can.

January 18

Serve only the Lord your God and fear him alone. Obey his commands, listen to his voice, and cling to him.
~Deuteronomy 13:4

Satan desires to separate you from God and make you forget about both God's faithful character and His promises. Satan uses people in our lives to lead us astray and "down the wrong path." God tells us time and time again to be careful not to steer off His path, slipping into idolatry, or giving into temptation.

To cling is to hold tightly. We <u>must cling onto God and His word</u> even when there seems to be no way out, the pain is so deep, or we have lost nearly all hope. Don't give up the good fight of faith! Resist Satan and turn to your heavenly Father who's love for you is greater than you can comprehend.

Dear Lord,

Strengthen my faith and hope in You. Please give me discernment in knowing who is leading me on the path of righteousness and who is leading me on the path of destruction, further from you. When times are more than I feel like I can bare, keep me strong and don't let me loosen my grip on Your Word.

January 19

Give generously to the poor, not grudgingly, for the Lord your
God will bless you in everything you do.
~Deuteronomy 15:10

There will always be people who live in poverty because we
live in a fallen world. This is no excuse to treat them
indifferently. We should use our resources, time, and gifts to
enhance their well-being. Many people think of giving
financially when they hear "give" to those in need, but it is not
always about money. Give someone your time by simply
talking and/or being with them. Share a warm smile and hug
with someone in need of hope.

God has blessed each of us with gifts, talents, and strengths.
Help your neighbor fix his fence if you've repaired yours
previously, give your coworker advice on her new puppy if
you're knowledgeable in dog training, or help you friend edit
her resume if writing and grammar is a strength of yours. You
see? Money, food, clothes, and other material possessions are
not the only options to give to others. You can give your time
and share your strengths!

Pride, greed, and selfishness won't lead to lasting success or
true joy. Giving to those in need and thinking less of yourself
will greatly bless the receiver, but you also reap eternal
blessings! Let's make the world a better place by giving more.

Dear Jesus,

Show me how I can be more generous not just to the poor, but to my
family, friends, coworkers, and anyone you place in my path. I pray
that Your light shines through me when I give to and serve others so
that they can know you more.

January 20

The Lord has declared today that you are his people, his own special treasure, just as he promised, and that you must obey all his commands. ~Deuteronomy 26:18

At your point of salvation, you declare that you choose to follow Jesus in every aspect of your life. Meditate on this: "I am God's special treasure." When you truly grasp how incredible this fact is, you will undoubtedly be less likely to believe the enemy's lies that call you worthless and unloved.

All the Lord's promises are true and He has promised us that we are his own special treasure! His love for you is unconditional and unending. There is absolutely nothing you can do or not do to change that.

Dear Father,

Thank you for your unconditional love that You continue to pour into me day after day. I am blessed beyond belief to be called your special treasure. Your wonderful instructions are for my good and the good of everyone, so I choose to obey You above all. Thank you for being my faithful Father.

January 21

Wherever you go and whatever you do, you will be blessed.
~Deuteronomy 28:6

When you obey God without question, without doubt, and without concern, a blessing is sure to follow. If His Spirit convicts you to do/say something, obey! Even though it may seem ridiculous or make zero sense in your mind, TRUST Him and just do it. The Lord may be protecting you and/or someone else, strengthening part of your character, testing and growing your faith, and/or revealing important truths He wants you to learn.

God knows exactly what He is doing! We will tell a child to keep his hands away from flames or to steer clear from other dangerous situations. The child may have no idea why he was instructed this, but that doesn't mean he can't obey.

In the same way, if God gives us a command that doesn't make sense, we should not question, "Why?" We do not see the danger, but He does. Other times, God tells us to do something that appears absolutely crazy. Obey anyway because He could very well be enhancing your character and/or teaching you a valuable lesson. Furthermore, He gives us instructions that we don't understand to grow our faith. We are presented with a choice between God's path or our own (or someone else's), and He wants to see if we have faith in Him.

Dear Lord,

I will obey you when I don't understand why. I will go where you tell me to go even when I am comfortable where I am. I will say what you want me to say even when I am nervous to do so. I will follow your path even when I'm confused as to why you're leading me there. I will face my enemies and fears even when I'm terrified. I will obey because I trust You!

January 22

The lord will conquer your enemies when they attack you. They will attack you from one direction, but they'll scatter from you in seven! ~Deuteronomy 28:7

When someone strikes against you or the world around you seems to be caving in, remember the battle is the Lord's, and He is victorious! God has such a unique way of weaving positive circumstances through our battles. He brings peace from chaos, joy from sadness, victory from weakness, and light from the darkness!

Dear Father,

When I'm in the midst of a frightening battle, I will trust in your mighty power and wait in expectation as you drive my enemies away. Thank you for bringing good from evil.

January 23

Do not be afraid or discouraged, for the Lord will personally go ahead of you. He will be with you. He will neither fail you nor abandon you. ~Deuteronomy 31:8

Trying something new? Moving to a foreign place where you know no one? Diagnosed with a severe illness? Frightened or anxious all the time? Whatever the case, whisper "Jesus help me."

He is always at your side, <u>with you</u> through all your suffering. God sent Jesus to be a man on earth so he could experience pain, suffering, heartache, stress, hunger and thirst, anxiety, fear, and all the emotions we endure *so that* he can understand our hurt. He yearns to comfort you in these trying times. Call upon his name, and He will help! Unlike people, <u>Jesus will never fail you or abandon you</u>.

Dear Jesus,

Thank you for dying on the cross for my sins and giving me eternal life. You tell us that in this life we will have trouble, but to take heart since you have already won the victory by defeating death. When I am petrified, please give me courage. When I am anxious, please pour your perfect peace into my soul. When I am in great anguish, please provide relief and comfort. When my hope is running on empty, please refill my heart with faith!

January 24

I will proclaim the name of the Lord; how glorious is our God! ~Deuteronomy 32:3

Word of mouth is one of the fastest ways in which businesses gain more customers. When you have a fantastic experience at a restaurant or hotel, you naturally run to tell all your family and friends how amazing it was. When you watch an incredible movie or attend an outstanding concert, you can't wait to share with others how great it was. When you are blessed with a better career, car, or home, you enjoy sharing that success with others. Why are we so quick to tell everyone about these things and so hesitant to proclaim Jesus' name and share the gospel?

Those who have a personal relationship with Jesus still need to be reminded of His goodness, genuine compassion, and awe-inspiring miracles. We all become discouraged from time to time.

Those who have never heard of Jesus won't ever know about Him, develop a relationship with Him, or be saved unless we as Christians proclaim His name and teach them about the gospel! How will they know about Jesus unless someone leads them in His direction? Don't ever be nervous to talk about Jesus, your personal testimony, or the miracles you have witnessed.

Dear Lord,

As I go about today, show me who needs to know You, hear Your word, be encouraged by my testimony, or have their hope restored. Holy Spirit, please give me a soft, loving tone of voice and the exact words he/she needs to hear.

January 25

*He found them in a desert land, in an empty, howling
wasteland. He surrounded them and watched over them; he
guarded them as he would guard his own eyes.*
~Deuteronomy 32:10

Even if you're banished to the ends of the earth or alone deep
in the trenches out of everyone's sight, <u>God knows exactly
where you are</u>. He will wrap His loving arms around you,
watch over you, and guard you.

Maybe your own sin led you into the empty pit or maybe it
was the sin of others. Maybe the enemy got a hold of you, and
you believed his lies which led you to fall into his trap.

God will never put you in a situation you can't handle with
Him. He may have you in a frightening or overwhelming
scenario to give you the opportunity to cry out to Him,
remembering that you are not self-sufficient, but rather
completely dependent on Him.

Dear God,

*Thank you for being with me in the darkness. When I don't see a
way out, I know you are still there with me. Thank you for guarding
me from further harm and watching over me. I cry out to you right
now! I need you. I cannot go through life without you. Show me
what you're trying to teach me Lord and rescue me from this
despair.*

January 26

Be strong and very courageous. Be careful to obey all the instructions Moses gave you. Don't deviate from them, turning either to the left or to the right. Then you'll be successful in everything you do.
~Joshua 1:7

If you're putting something together, installing an appliance, or making a fancy recipe, would you delete a step? Would you add your own steps? Would you change the order of the steps? Would you manipulate them in any way or twist them around? Absolutely not – you would follow the instructions, hopefully.

Think about what would happen if you deleted, added to, changed the order, or manipulated the steps…. the furniture wouldn't be set up right or work right, the appliance wouldn't function properly, and the recipe would yield poor results!

When you know what God commands and wants, obey His instructions exactly as they are. Don't delete part of the instructions or add to them. Don't change the order of his steps. Don't manipulate or twist His instructions around. Every single word in God's command is there for a specific reason. Success, blessings, and prosperity will come when we obey God precisely and trust Him wholeheartedly.

Notice this verse opens with "be strong and very courageous." There will be times when obeying God requires great bravery on our part because He may be telling us to leave our comfort zone or face our fear. Notice it also says "be careful to obey." We must be careful and on guard because the enemy will tempt us and try to lead us away from God's word.

Dear God,

Thank you for your wonderful instructions. I know that Your word teaches me to live righteously and protects me from falling prey to the enemy. Lord, keep me strong and courageous so that I never hesitate to obey You.

January 27

The lord said to Joshua, "Get up! Why are you lying on your face like this?" ~Joshua 7:10

Is anxiety plaguing your mind? Is there terror at your doorstep this very moment? Do you have difficulty maintaining or mending relationships? Are you exhausted? Are you enduring a major illness?

Look to God above, who's full of compassion for you, and arise! Despite the fact you may feel miserable or afraid, you can choose to look up. Go to a quiet place alone and pour out your heart to Him. He is fully prepared to answer your prayers.

Dear God,

Hear my cry right now. Help me move when I feel like I can't. Help me be brave when I am afraid. Please give me some relief from this pain and suffering. I need you, Father. I need your love, peace, joy, comfort, and strength.

January 28

"You are a witness to your own decision," Joshua said. "You have chosen to serve the Lord." ~Joshua 24:22

When you develop a pure, intimate relationship with God, you are your own witness! Don't ever forget that YOU chose to serve the Lord, so continuously communicate with Him, asking what He wants you to do, and then obey with a grateful attitude.

Believing that Jesus is the Son of God and choosing Him as your savior is the best decision you will ever make. When you make this choice, you are choosing to serve Him.

Dear God,

Humble my heart. Show me how I can best serve You through serving others. Point out to me those in my home, workplace, and community that I can help. I pray that when I serve, others are drawn to Your light that shines through me.

January 29

*Whenever the lord raised up a judge over Israel, he was with
that judge and rescued the people from their enemies
throughout the judge's lifetime. For the lord took pity on his
people, who were burdened by oppression and suffering.*
~Judges 2:18

To "take pity" means to have compassion, deep sympathy,
mercy and tenderness. God knows exactly what you're going
through - the burdens, oppression, and suffering. His
unending love for you rescues you from distress.
Remember that.

Dear Father,

*Thank you for your unconditional love that you exude every moment
of every day. I am in awe of your magnificent glory and limitless
love. When I am mistreated, helpless, hurt, or burdened I cry to you
for You alone can rescue me. Thank you, Father, for comforting me,
coming to my aide, healing my pain, and removing my burdens.*

January 30

"Listen, you kings! Pay attention, you mighty rulers! For I will sing to the Lord. I will make music to the Lord, the God of Israel!" ~Judges 5:3

When you are joyful, sing to your amazing God! When you're thankful and blessed, praise Him! Don't hold back your love song to Him. Shout His name for all to hear.

It's important to remember to praise God during hard times as well. It is possible to have joy in the midst of a negative situation. How? By fixing your eyes on Jesus and reminding yourself of His promises, you are then able experience His peace. The Lord is incredibly close to the brokenhearted, and to all who cry out His name because of His deep compassion for us.

Dear Lord,

I praise your name in both good times and bad. You are in control and work out all things for good. Thank you for this opportunity for me to worship you and proclaim your glory!

January 31

So, God caused water to gush out of a hollow in the ground at Lehi, and Samson was revived as he drank. Then he named that place "The Spring of the One Who Cried Out," and it's still in Lehi to this day.
~Judges 15:19

In a deep, passionate prayer, Samson cried to the Lord to be replenished because he was terribly thirsty. God responded immediately. We worship that same God today. Our Father is the same yesterday, today, tomorrow, and forever. Pray genuinely and passionately to God, asking Him whatever you need, and wait in expectation for His answer.

Dear Lord,

I am crying out to You today for replenishment. My soul longs for You more than anything – for Your love, comfort, peace, and joy. I will wait in hopeful expectation for Your response, and even though I may not like the answer, I know Your way is best and I will follow wherever You lead.

February 1

May the Lord, the God of Israel, under whose wings you have come to take refuge, reward you fully for what you have done.
~Ruth 2:12

Ruth was a kind, loyal, hard working woman who left her home town to glean in the fields among strangers. Boaz, the wealthy landowner, noticed her strong work ethic and told his workers to be generous to her.

Ruth was greatly rewarded for her faithfulness, love, and serving heart. Boaz married her and they had a son, Obed, who was king David's grandfather. Ruth is one of only five women mentioned in Jesus' genealogy.

The story of Ruth shows how God works in the ordinary for those who trust Him and that faithfulness leads to eternal blessings.

Dear Lord,

Thank you for the ordinary tasks and the day to day routines. I know that you create extraordinary situations from ordinary people. Thank you for blessing me beyond what I deserve.

February 2

No one is holy like the Lord! There is no one besides you;
there is no Rock like our God.
~1 Samuel 2:2

In this prayer of praise, Hannah declares how holy and
wonderful our God is.

For years, Peninnah continuously taunted Hannah because
Peninnah had children, but Hannah did not. The constant
ridicule led Hannah to cry out to the Lord. Eli witnessed this
and blessed her. The Bible says "In due time, she gave birth to
a son." Hannah went from being infertile to having 3 sons and
2 daughters because she was faithful with her first child
Samuel.

A coworker might insult or mock you day after day. A family
member or friend may put you down time and time again.
You may be in distress for months or years. Whatever the case
and however long it's been, remember to pour your heart out
to the Lord. He rewards faithfulness and devotion to Him.

Dear Father,

You are my fortress whom I put my trust in. When I am wounded, I
will cry out to you because I know you not only hear my prayers, but
will help me persevere in the time between my prayer and Your
answer.

February 3

But be sure to fear the Lord and faithfully serve him. Think of all the wonderful things he has done for you.
~1 Samuel 12:24

Samuel encouraged the people of Israel to not be afraid. He reassured them that although they sinned greatly, if they repented from their wicked ways and sought God wholeheartedly, the Lord will rescue them yet again. God will never abandon his people, even if His people abandon Him. Samuel reminds them to think about all the wonderful things God has done for them in the past.

We can really take this to heart. Even though we fall short, sin, and make some major mistakes, we can rest because without a shadow of a doubt, if we choose to repent of our sins and genuinely turn to God, He will come to our aide. He will repair our mistakes and turn our failures into learning opportunities and success stories.

Always reminisce on what God has given you, done for you, protected you from, healed you of, and helped you through. He deserves all the glory.

Dear Father,

Thank You for everything I have, for I know it all comes from You. Thank You for guiding me through tough situations. Thank You for Your continuous protection and healing. To You be the glory!

February 4

*God told Samuel, "Don't judge by his appearance or height,
for I rejected him. The lord doesn't see things the way you see
them. People judge by outward appearance,
but the lord looks at the heart."*
~1 Samuel 16:7

The next time you find yourself judging another person based
on their appearance, remember that you are a child of God
and you should strive to live like Him. *God looks at the heart,* so
that is where you should look as well.

Every single person has been born for their unique purpose
and journey. We each have our own experiences. We have
absolutely no right to judge anyone on how they look. Choose
to look past what's visible. Focus on others' acts of kindness,
words of affirmation, and genuine respect and love they
demonstrate to others.

Don't fall into the comparison trap either. Comparing yourself
to others leads you down a terrible road of insecurity, low
self-esteem, shame, guilt, and sadness. You are a child of the
Almighty God! The most important view of yourself is not
how others view you, or even yourself for that matter. The
way God sees you, as a remarkable, beautiful, spectacular
child, is what matters most.

Dear God,

Thank you for giving us the prime example of looking at the heart. Help me to see past the visible. If I begin to judge someone, stop me. Remind me that I don't know what they're going through. Cleanse both my heart and mind so that I do not compare my appearance, opportunities, material possessions, etc. to that of others. Shift my way of thinking from paying attention to how someone looks to focusing on his/her heart.

February 5

Now go and say to my servant David, 'This is what the Lord of Heaven's Armies has declared: I took you from tending sheep in the pasture and selected you to be the leader of my people Israel.' ~2 Samuel 7:8

The Lord instructed Nathan the prophet to give this uplifting word from Him. God enjoys taking regular people who demonstrate faithfulness and devotion to Him and elevating them to a position of influence. God takes them from a place of being led to a place of leading.

If you're feeling stuck in a seemingly mundane job, remain faithful and continue working hard. Even the simplest of tasks are noted by God. When you are faithful in the small things, He will bless you with more! Remember that the blessing isn't just for you, but for His purposes and the advancement of His kingdom.

Furthermore, everyone has the potential to lead someone else in one way or another. We can use our personal experiences to help guide and advise others.

Dear Lord,

I am Your servant. I am simply passing by here on Earth until I reach my permanent home in heaven. While here, please give me the wisdom to lead those You call me to lead.

February 6

God's way is perfect. All the Lord's promises prove true. He is a shield for all who look to him for protection.
~2 Samuel 22:31

David learned that God's way is unquestionably perfect. His promises never fail. He is a shield that can protect you from every kind of attack.

The only one you can always and completely depend on is God! He is more secure and capable than any person. Place your faith in Him. No matter how bumpy the road ahead appears to be, when you are on God's path, there is nothing to worry about. Yes, there may be hardships and pain on His path, but He is with you every step of the way, helping you and creating a testimony that you will share with others in the future to comfort them.

Dear God,

Thank you for your fully reliable promises. I rest my faith in your flawless character. Father, you are my steady safeguard whom I can always run to. You are supreme and I joyfully praise your name above all names!

February 7

*Give me an understanding heart so that I can govern your
people well and know the difference between right and wrong.*
~1 Kings 3:9

The Lord asked Solomon what he wanted, and Solomon's
request for an understanding heart pleased God so much that
He joyfully granted his wish. He gave Solomon a wise <u>and</u>
understanding heart as no one else had or ever will have. He
wanted wisdom to lead God's people well and help them.
Because of his selfless request, in addition to immense
wisdom, God blessed Solomon with riches, fame, success, and
prosperity.

We make thousands of choices each and every day. Whether
we like it or not, we need God's help in making decisions both
large and small. Our life would be more "smooth sailing" if
we could confidently make a decision while knowing it was
the right one. In order to have such confidence, we need the
Lord's wisdom.

Dear God,

*Please give me a wise and understanding heart so that I can have the
discernment to make wise choices. Even if the decision isn't
something I want to do, but in my heart I know it's wise, I will obey
You because I trust wherever You lead me.*

February 8

Solomon prayed, "O lord, God of Israel, there's no God like you in all of heaven above or on the earth below. You keep your covenant and show unfailing love to all who walk before you in wholehearted devotion."
~1 Kings 8:23

Halleluiah, God's love never fails! His compassionate love for us is the same when we sin over and over again, choose the wrong path, and abandon His will and go our own way. He keeps every single promise He makes and stands at the ready with mercy, grace, forgiveness, and *love* for all those who turn back to Him in wholehearted devotion.

Don't lose enthusiasm for seeking God, worshiping Him, and praying. The Lord searches the whole earth for those whose hearts are completely dedicated to Him, and He blesses them beyond belief!

Dear Father,

Thank you for loving me when I am broken, when I sin, and when I leave Your path. Jesus, soak my heart and keep my faith in you strong. When fatigue sets in, fuel me with energy. When discouragement comes, uplift me from my sorrow. Help me continue moving forward one step at a time.

February 9

*May he give us the desire to do his will in everything and to
obey all the commands, decrees, and regulations
that he gave our ancestors.*
~1 Kings 8:58

It can definitely be hard desiring something other than what
we want. Our insignificant minds desire things that aren't in
line with God's will. We must continuously ask for His help to
transform our thinking to not only accept His will, but to live
it out whole heartedly.

Dear God,

*You know my dreams, goals, plans, and my hearts' desires, but
ultimately, I want what You want. If my dreams and goals don't
align with your will, please instill the dreams You have for me into
my soul. If my heart's desires aren't what you have planned for me,
please change them. Change my desires to your desires. Help me to
let go of anything that is blocking me from Your blessings.*

February 10

A warrior putting on his sword for battle shouldn't boast like a warrior who's already won.
~1 Kings 20:11

Be on guard against bragging as though you've already won (landed that job, came in first place at the marathon, defeated your opponents) because God frowns upon that kind of egotism. Pride is evidence of selfishness. There is nothing wrong with being proud of your accomplishments, but Jesus instructs us repeatedly to remain humble. The only thing we can boast about is how awesome, powerful, loving, and good our Lord and Savior is!

Plus, we don't always win the battle, so why brag as though we are already victorious? We win and lose in life. Losses and trials are actually wonderful learning opportunities. God may allow defeat, tragedy, and stress in our lives so that we learn an important lesson, become more dependent on Him, and/or become more humble.

Dear God,

Keep my lips from bragging. Keep my heart humble and pure. Thank you for the wins and losses in my life. I know that it is all for my benefit and for the benefit of those around me, for You are a good, good Father.

February 11

She said to her husband, "I am sure this man who stops in from time to time is a holy man of God."
~2 Kings 4:9

A woman from Shunem was "sure" – certain, confident, convinced – that Elisha was a prophet of God. Because of her steady faith and total belief, God blessed her with a son (she didn't have any children & her husband was old).

Unfortunately, the boy died, but the woman stood firm in her faith yet again. She noticed Elisha in town and refused to go home without him. Once home, Elisha went in alone where the boy was lying and miraculously breathed life into him! The child sneezed seven times (7 represents spiritual perfection) and opened his eyes!

Don't let your faith waver. God is perfect, all powerful, and in complete control. His love never fails and His promises are unbreakable. Therefore, you can be absolutely certain in Him. You can trust Him without an ounce of doubt!

Dear God,

I trust in You – in Your ways, timing, and will. I am certain that You hear my requests and cries for help because I know that You have compassion for me. Thank you for all the blessings I can see and even those I don't see. I praise your glorious name!

February 12

"Don't be afraid!" Elisha told him.
"For there are more on our side than on theirs!"
~2 Kings 6:16

Elisha's servant was petrified when he saw the Aramean army approaching. Elisha had no fear at all because he trusted completely that God would help and protect him, and that is exactly what happened! The Lord opened the servant's eyes so he could see that indeed there were troops and chariots of fire on their side. God blinded the Arameans and Elisha led them (his enemies) to the middle of Samaria!

The most repeated command in the Bible is to not be afraid. God knows how much we tremble in frightening situations, worry in uncertainty, and fear both what we can and cannot see, which is why we need the reminder to not be afraid. If you're in a situation where victory seems impossible, trust God anyway! He is working mysteriously behind the curtain. If you don't see a solution or are so scared of what you see approaching, relax and lean on God because He is always right there with you.

Dear God,

When my confidence and faith begin to falter, I will redirect my mind to Your promises! When I begin to anticipate the worst, I will remember You are for me and will work everything out for good. When I begin to fear or worry, I will remember that You are in full control.

February 13

"Remember, O Lord, how I have always been faithful to you and have served you single-mindedly, always doing what pleases you." Then he broke down and wept bitterly.
~2 Kings 20:3

Hezekiah became deathly ill. The prophet Isaiah told him that he will die soon. Upon hearing this, he cried to his Father. Because Hezekiah let it all out by breaking down and sobbing before the Lord, he was healed 3 days later! God rescued him and the entire city from the king of Assyria!

Rather than complaining about your illness (or whatever problem you are currently facing), *surrender yourself fully to God.* Cry out to your Healer who soothes your soul and rescues you.

Dear God,

Hear my cry. I give up. I surrender myself and my situation to you right now. I need you, Father. You are the one who can heal my broken heart and give me peace. I choose to lean on Your love. I surrender everything to You. Oh Father, hear my cry.

February 14

And David became more and more powerful because the lord
of heaven's armies was with him.
~1 Chronicles 11:9

When God's angels are your army, <u>nothing</u> can stop you. You
will be fully capable to handle any situation! When a problem
arises, God will either handle it himself or equip you with
exactly what you need to deal with it. David's kingship was
God's choice, not David's or the peoples.

No one, no illness, no disaster, no tragedy, no problem, and no
battle will prevail against God's specific purpose for you. Pick
up your cross and follow Jesus, obeying all His commands
and trusting in Him, and the Lord of heaven's armies will be
with you just like they were with David.

Dear Jesus,

Thank you for fighting for me! You are my strength. I know that no
matter how hard things may get, your angels guard me night and
day. Thank you for your persistent protection.

February 15

Sing to him; yes, sing his praises.
Tell everyone about his wonderful deeds.
~1 Chronicles 16:9

It is crucial to remember God's marvelous deeds. Everyone becomes discouraged at times, which is why we need to reflect on the blessings He's given us and the amazing ways He came through for us.

Sing praises to His name so that others can be uplifted, too. Tell everyone (friends, family, coworkers, and acquaintances) how good your heavenly Father is.

You never know when your message about God's greatness can profoundly impact someone else! Someone may be in desperate need for just a little bit of hope, and your testimony keeps them from falling into despair. Someone could be terribly depressed, and your words infuse just enough joy in their hearts to feel better. Someone could be in deep pain, and your story gives them comfort and relief.

Dear God,

Help me to remember all that you've blessed me. Remind me of the miracles You've performed and immaculate wonders you've shown me. Give me the confidence to boldly praise your name to everyone. I pray that my experiences can encourage others and lead them to you!

February 16

Search for the lord and his strength. Continually seek him.
~1 Chronicles 16:11

Notice the word *continually*. This does not mean to seek Him just at church on Sundays or only during hard times.

<u>Gaze to Him always</u>, regardless of your circumstances. It's so important to *remember* His track record – how many times he forgave you, helped you, and blessed you.

Dear Lord,

You are my fortress; my unshakable foundation. Therefore, I will seek Your strength. Lord, I pray that the Holy Spirit reminds me to seek You whenever my mind wanders elsewhere. You have helped me in the past, will help me right now during this struggle, and will help me in my future trials. I believe in Your power and trust in You!

February 17

But who am I, and who are my people, that we could give anything to you? Everything we have has come from you, and we give you only what you first gave us!
~1 Chronicles 29:14

David's prayer of praise exalted God's glory and served to dedicate the offerings given for building the temple. David recognized that everything one owns is God given.

Your possessions, career, abilities, and talents <u>all come from God.</u> Success, honor, and prosperity all come from Him as well. We must always remember to thank Him often for everything we have, for He blessed us with it all. Be grateful that He made you His unique and wonderful treasure!

Dear Father,

You are worthy of all praise! Thank you for creating me the way I am. I truly am blessed. Thank you for my unique abilities and talents, but also for my weaknesses. With you, my weaknesses can turn into strengths. Thank you for everyone you've placed in my life including those who are always there and those who come & go. Thank you for the shoes on my feet and roof over my head. Thank you for absolutely everything.

February 18

Then if my people who are called by my name will humble themselves and pray and seek my face and turn from their wicked ways, I will hear from heaven and will forgive their sins and restore their land.
~2 Chronicles 7:14

We all mess up. We fall short in our personal relationships with others, in our jobs, and in the goals we set for ourselves.

We are sinners. The good news is that our Lord always forgives! His mercy overflows and He is full of sympathy for us even when we are at our worst.

All you need to do is recognize your sin and repent - turn the other way and pray to God for forgiveness.

Dear Father,

Thank you for your unending grace that you pour onto me, no questions asked. I am in awe of how tenderhearted and forgiving you are! I will do my best to live righteously and obey all your commands. When I slip up, I will turn to You for forgiveness and cleansing once again. Thank you for loving me even when I fail.

February 19

"I didn't believe what was said until I arrived here and saw it with my own eyes. In fact, I had not heard the half of your great wisdom! It is far beyond what I was told."
~2 Chronicles 9:6

The Queen of Sheba heard of Solomon's fame, but didn't believe it until she witnessed his great wisdom for herself. We are similar, not believing things until we see them with our own eyes.

One thing you don't have to "see" with your eyes to believe is that GOD IS REAL. Faith is the confident belief in what you don't literally see. Those who call Jesus their Savior believe that he died on the cross for our sins and rose from the dead. If we have strong faith in that seemingly unimaginable miracle, why is it so difficult for us to have faith that God will answer a prayer?

Dear God,

I don't want to be the person who only believes something if it is physically seen. Please give me a stable faith that does not fluctuate when hard times come. Lord, remove all worries and fears that hinder my faith. I know You will answer this prayer, so I thank you in advance.

February 20

Then Jehoshaphat added,
"But first, let's find out what the Lord says."
~2 Chronicles 18:4

Jehoshaphat, a faithful king of Judah, trusted the Lord throughout his life. He made some poor choices, but here he checked with God first, which is what we ought to do as well.

Never rush into something! Even if it *feels* perfect to you, is just what you've been longing for, or it just seems "right," always talk to God first. Before you talk to your spouse, closest friend, mentor, or whoever it is who deeply trust, go to God because He knows you better than you know yourself. He is perfect and unquestionable. You can never go wrong when you seek Him!

Dear God,

I am confused. I need help making this decision. I need guidance in which direction YOU want me to take. Holy Spirit, give me clarity on this situation. Advise me on what YOU want me to do and where YOU want me to go. I desire to do Your will above my own, so I am asking that You grant me the blessing of discernment and wisdom in making this decision. Thank you!

February 21

*Fear the Lord and judge with integrity, for the Lord our God
does not tolerate perverted justice, partiality,
or the taking of bribes.*
~2 Chronicles 19:7

We must be aware of the temptation to judge. Remember that
we serve God, the one true judge. He is indisputable. God
blesses those who honor others and demonstrate integrity.

Dear Father,

*Remove anything in my mind, heart, or soul that keeps me from
showing integrity. I am sorry for judging others because I have
absolutely no right to judge anyone. Take away the habit of judging.
I strive to please You above all. Help me to see others as You see
them.*

February 22

"O our God, won't you stop them? We are powerless against this mighty army that is about to attack us. We do not know what to do, but we are looking to you for help."
~2 Chronicles 20:12

King Jehoshaphat responded to the news of war with praying to God. Even though he was unsure of what exactly to do, he did exactly what he should have – looked up to God in heaven and sought *His help*.

Even if an attack is imminent and you feel completely helpless, direct your gaze above! If you are in a raging war and success seems impossible, turn to God! Relinquish control to Him. If He tells you to move, go forth. If He asks you to be still, don't move. Either way, trust in Him and watch as He fights for you.

Dear God,

You are my fighter! Thank you for conquering my enemies who try to attack me and for keeping me safeguarded against the evil that is all around. If you want me to act, I will obey. If you want me to be still, I will stop all of my plans and give you control.

February 23

*And Azariah the high priest, from the family of Zadok,
replied, "Since the people began bringing their gifts to the
Lord's Temple, we have had enough to eat and plenty to spare.
The Lord has blessed his people, and all this is left over."*
~2 Chronicles 31:10

King Hezekiah gave thanks and praise to the Lord at the gates
of the Temple. The people of Israel generously gave portions
of their goods to show their devotion to God. The blessing that
came from their tithes was much greater than they
anticipated! They had enough to eat and plenty to spare from
spring to autumn.

When we tithe and give generously, whether it's financially,
giving our time to serve others, or using our strengths to help
others, we are demonstrating our trust in the Lord and
showing our commitment to Him. The Lord loves to bestow
blessings upon cheerful givers. Furthermore, more often than
not, His blessings will overflow and be so amazing that you
are left in deep awe of His generosity.

Dear Lord,

*Thank you for blessing me beyond what I deserve. Show me how I
can be even more generous and how I can use what you've given me
to help others. Jesus, make me become a cheerful and generous giver.*

February 24

"He may have a great army, but they are merely men. We have the lord our God to help us and to fight our battles for us!" Hezekiah's words greatly encouraged the people.
~2 Chronicles 32:8

Hezekiah explained to his men that although the king of Assyria has a mighty army, there is a supreme, unequaled power on their side!

Your whole family or circle of friends might be against you. Everyone at your workplace might continually taunt or disrespect you. You may feel defeated before the battle has even taken place.

Do not worry because a stronger power is on your side. God and His angels will take care of you.

Dear God,

You are sovereign. Your skill is unmatched and your knowledge is sound! Thank you for being on my side in both minor problems and huge obstacles I cannot face alone. I will not worry because Your love for me is secure and your protection of me is certain.

February 25

The lord, the God of their ancestors, repeatedly sent his
prophets to warn them, for he had compassion
on his people and his Temple.
~2 Chronicles 36:15

He <u>repeatedly</u> warned his people. Even though they
continued to sin, He <u>always forgave</u> them when they repented
and warned them out of love. He showed them the right path.

We either don't see his warning signs, or, we do see them and
choose to disobey. God will continue to pursue us. Observe
and attend to the warnings or don't. Following Him is our
choice.

Your unyielding God loves you beyond measure and knows
you better than you know yourself, and that alone should tell
you what to choose – His path.

Dear Father,

I am sorry for ignoring your warnings and going my own way
despite knowing it's not where You want me to go. I know in my
heart that Your plans are <u>for me</u>. Forgive me for not listening to
You. Holy Spirit, help me resist my flesh and instead listen to God
my Father.

February 26

Praise Him for demonstrating such unfailing love by honoring me before the king, his council, and his mighty nobles. I'm encouraged because God's gracious hand is on me.
~Ezra 7:28

Ezra immediately directs his focus and thanksgiving to his gracious Father. Stay positive and hopeful even during dark times because God's gracious hand is right on you, just as it was on Ezra. The light of Jesus shines in the darkest of places, so call upon his name "Help me Jesus."

Dear Jesus,

Your unfailing love and grace rescue me from despair. You are the Light of the world that shines brightly in my darkness. When my view is obstructed and I have lost nearly all hope, there You are comforting me in Your arms and infusing hope into my soul. Thank you Jesus!

February 27

You gave them bread from heaven when they were hungry and water from the rock when they were thirsty. You commanded them to go and take possession of the land you had sworn to give them.
~Nehemiah 9:15

There may come a time in life when you literally run out of resources or lose everything. Anxiety and fear make a home within you because you don't know how you're going to provide for yourself or family. Stress and discouragement entangle you because you have no idea where or how you can find food or shelter. You see no solution, no relief, no freedom.

Lift your head up, gazing to heaven, and cry out to God who is your Provider. He does the unthinkable! Our God sends blessings, performs miracles, and creates things including life itself *out of nothing*. In an instant, He can send you *exactly what you need*. Believe that He can and have faith (believe in what you cannot see) that He will. He extends His limitless resources at just the perfect time. Trust in Him.

Dear Heavenly Father,

I am completely out of resources and cannot see or find a solution, so I need Your help to make me look beyond what's visibly in front of me and towards heaven instead. Only You can perform a miracle in an instant, sending me what I need when no one else can and providing for me when there is nothing. I trust in Your ways because I know You have compassion for me and have plans to prosper me. Thank You Father for this opportunity to trust you more.

February 28

But in your great mercy you did not abandon them to die in the wilderness. The pillar of cloud still led them forward by day, and the pillar of fire showed them the way through the night.
~Nehemiah 9:19

Even though the people disobeyed God and were stubborn, He was merciful and always with them. He guided them, sent the Holy Spirit to instruct them, and provided enough food and water for them to be sustained for forty years in the wilderness.

God is always with you and will never forsake you, even when you disobey or walk away from Him. He is the perfect guide because He knows every danger and detour on the map. Threats and danger certainly can cause us to be afraid or panic, but just call Jesus' name and remember his command "Be strong and courageous for I am with you."

If you're following Jesus, you can relax even in frightening times because His path is the way to *life*.

We will have many detours in life – people, situations, or circumstances that reroute us. Often, we become angry that we can't reach our destination/goal/dream quickly and in the way we wanted, or discouraged that our trip is prolonged.

Again, relax if you're walking with Jesus. His detours are strategically placed in your life. Trust where He is leading you!

Dear God,

*I may not always know where I'm headed, but I know You do!
Terror and panic may set in when I come across danger, but I will
quickly call upon Your name and remember Your command to "be
strong and courageous for I am with you." I may become
discouraged or angry when I reach a detour, but I will obey the
direction because You are all knowing! Thank you for being by my
side at all times. I trust where You are leading me.*

March 1

And as news of the king's decree reached all the provinces, there was great mourning among the Jews. They fasted, wept, and wailed, and many people lay in burlap and ashes.
~Esther 4:3

The powerful official Haman was furious when Mordecai, a Jew, refused to bow down to him. This led to Haman to persuade King Xerxes to destroy all Jews. When the Jewish community heard that the king's decree to kill them was in effect, they fasted and cried their hearts out.

When you hear tragic news, what do you resort to? Who do you turn to? Only God himself is able to completely turn an impossible situation around. Seek Him first.

Dear Lord,

When terrible news reaches my ears, rather than quickly lash out in anger or grief, I will cry to You because I know you can reverse any situation. I praise Your triumphant name!

March 2

The king took off his signet ring – which he had taken back from Haman – and gave it to Mordecai. And Esther appointed Mordecai to be in charge of Haman's property.
~Esther 8:2

Although God's name is not mentioned in the book of Esther, one can definitely notice how God providentially cares for his people and orchestrates events to accomplish His purpose. Haman's evil plan to kill all the Jews backfired on him. Esther, once an orphan, became Queen of Persia. God used her to reveal Haman's plot and rescue His people.

This verse is significant because the same signet ring Haman used to seal the decree to murder all Jewish people was now given to Mordecai, the Jew he wanted to destroy the most. God will always protect His beloved children and His good will always prevails.

Dear Lord,

Thank you for your constant protection from my enemies. Even if I am surrounded by evil, I know You will deliver me from that terror. Thank you for taking what is meant to harm me and transforming it into something positive that benefits me. Although I do not always understand, I trust in Your ways.

March 3

The lord gave me what I had, and the lord has taken it away.
Praise the name of the lord!
~Job 1:21

Job was a righteous man whom God allowed Satan to test. When Satan struck Job's household, Job replied with worship, praising the Lord.

Have you ever questioned God saying, "Lord, why did you give me such a wonderful gift and then snatch it away from me!?" The gift you're referring to can be a job, home, spouse, child, financial blessing, or anything you had been desiring/asking for.

God doesn't take things away to punish or curse us. There are many reasons why He may bless you with something that leaves you. Consider that God wants to draw you closer to Him, teach you or someone else a lesson, transform your attitude or thoughts, demonstrate His power and glory, or give someone else hope because when they see us respond with praise during trials, they certainly gain a new perspective.

Dear Father,

Although it is challenging and sometimes painful losing a blessing, I understand You have a reason behind it. I may not know why, but I know You do, and I trust you. Help me to view times of hardship as opportunities for spiritual growth.

March 4

Should we accept only good things from the hand of God and never anything bad? So, in all this, Job said nothing wrong.
~Job 2:10

Job accepted the good and bad (terrible illness), which demonstrates his righteousness and faith.

Accept everything God delivers to you – the good, the outstanding, the terrible, the frightening, the stressful, etc.

He uses everything to work together in His intricate web for good for all those who trust and obey Him. If you're having a rough time accepting negative things, ask God to renew your mind. Praise Him no matter what cards you've been dealt!

Dear Lord,

I accept both the good and bad things in my life. Please revitalize my spirit when I am weary, turn my negative attitude into a positive one, and refocus my attention on Your loving presence. Help me to take my eyes off the problem and onto You. Lord, Your will is the safest place to be and I trust Your ways.

March 5

If I were you, I'd go to God and present my case to Him.
~Job 5:8

Three of Job's friends came to comfort and mourn with him as he let out his profound sadness from the suffering he endured. His friend Eliphaz encouraged him to go to God because of His countless miracles.

Who do you go to first for advice? Your spouse? Your mother or father? Your best friend? For everything we seek, question, or have concern for, the very first person we should talk to is GOD. Present your case to the Lord. Talk to Him, sharing your thoughts and feelings. Yes, He already knows your thoughts, and He knows what you'll say before you even utter a word, but the Lord delights in listening to your voice and <u>He wants to hear you.</u>

Dear Lord,

I come to you with open arms. You tell us to cast our burdens upon your shoulders, so here they are Father. Take my pain, heartache, stress, anxiety, and fear away in Jesus name. Fill me with peace and joy. Infuse strength into my weak bones that won't seem to move. Thank you for comforting me during my sorrows.

March 6

He will once again fill your mouth with laughter and
your lips with shouts of joy!
~Job 8:21

If you ever feel depressed and hopeless, impaired or incurable, overworked and exasperated, or heartbroken and heavy hearted – remember this truth! The Lord WILL bring joy, laughter, and peace back to you.

It can be extremely challenging to think positively when you're in the midst of suffering. Believe that the Lord will infuse joy within you once again.

Having a thankful mindset helps redirect your mind from negativity. Remember that the battle you're in is only temporary. Keep your eyes fixed on Jesus and be on the lookout for His ways. Expect to see the ashes turn into something beautiful because that is God's specialty.

Dear Father,

Even though I may go through pain and sorrow, I trust in this promise that You will bring joy to my heart once again. Keep my faith steady and my hope alive as I endure trials, trusting in You alone. I know you are using this battle for good. Teach me what You want me to learn and keep my eyes open wide so that I can see how You are turning this mess into a miracle.

March 7

He does great things too marvelous to understand. He performs countless miracles.
~Job 9:10

We often miss miracles that are happening right in our own homes, schools, work places, church, and communities because we have blinders over our eyes or ear plugs in our ears!

Each day, ask the Holy Spirit to empower you with spiritual eyes and ears so that you can be more open to the miracles God performs every single day.

Dear Lord,

I praise your mighty name! Keep me attuned to Your amazing miracles in my personal life as well as in the lives of those around me. Father, even when I don't understand, I choose to trust in You because Your ways are perfect.

March 8

But true wisdom and power are found in God;
counsel and understanding are his.
~Job 12:13

You can study day and night, be the expert in your field, or have the highest IQ in the world…. none of that intelligence comes even close to the wisdom of our mighty God! His thinking and reasoning are simply unfathomable.

Study the Truth to the best of your ability, soaking in as much knowledge about our mystifying, glorious God as possible!

Dear God,

I am in awe of your transcendent wisdom! Lord above all, help me be more attentive to Your word and voice. Teach me how I can be more discerning in my personal choices, profession, relationships, and spiritual walk. Please give me a greater understanding with a heavenly perspective. Thank you.

March 9

He uncovers mysteries hidden in darkness;
he brings light to the deepest gloom.
~Job 12:22

Even if you're stuck in a bottomless pit so dark that you can't see your hands or you're going through the most horrific storm of your life, Jesus Christ can and does bring His light and peace into that very place! Sometimes we have to hit rock bottom to witness his radiant light.

Change your perspective. Instead of being focused on the darkness, *think* of what God is doing or has there. God works in such mysterious ways, especially during extremely difficult times. Your hardship can be a blessing in disguise. A mystery is hidden there in the dark, like hidden treasure.

Dear Jesus,

Thank you for being my Savior and Light of the world. Even in my darkest place, Your light shines and gives me hope and provides a sense of security. Don't let fear take over when I'm in darkness. Give me confidence to trust You in the hopeless, grim, darkened days.

March 10

Now summon me, and I'll answer!
Or let me speak to you, and you reply.
~Job 13:22

Job is talking honestly and sincerely to God here, deeply desiring to communicate with Him. We should approach our Father with such humility and honesty as well, with our <u>hearts and minds fully open to whatever He has to say</u> and *waiting in expectation* for His reply.

It is impossible for God to lie. He promises that He will answer when we pray, so He will. Don't ever doubt Him! He may not answer on your terms or in your timing, but thank goodness for that because He is our Holy Creator who sees *every detail* in the big picture. His ways and timing are always best.

Dear God,

I come humbly before You today with my requests. Father, please give me an open mind and heart so I can know what Your answer is. My greatest desire is to live by Your will because I know that You have my best interest in mind and that Your plans work into an intricate, beautiful design.

March 11

*Submit to God, and you will have peace;
then things will go well for you. ~Job 22:21*

The Lord's tranquil, soothing peace that resides within you does not compare to anything in the world. Disaster and chaos can be right outside your door and yet you *feel* a deep sense of calmness. People are surprised that not only are you coping quite well with such a terrible circumstance, but you are *content and at peace with a thankful attitude.* This is the perfect opportunity for you to talk about your magnificent Savior because only Jesus can bestow such a profound peace within your soul.

Everyone who loves the Lord with all their heart, mind, and soul, and who submits to Him, can access His peace at any moment.

Dear Jesus,

Thank you for trials and stressful times. These are opportunities for me to seek Your peace that resides within me. Lord, remove any obstacle that blocks me from finding that peace within.

March 12

So, he will do to me whatever he has planned.
~Job 23:14

Stop worrying about getting that promotion or job. Stop
analyzing what would happen if you did or didn't
date/marry that person. Stop trying to plan every detail of
certain areas of your life.

Relinquish the desire to control situations and others. God's
plan will prevail regardless of what you do, say, or think. It is
not enough to merely accept God's will. We are to
continuously chase after it and remain grateful even when it
differs from our desires or plans.

Dear God,

*Help me to stop being fixated on planning. I surrender all of my
plans and to-do lists to You. Holy Spirit, draw me closer to the
Father so I can know what His plans are. I want to follow His steps
and check off tasks on His to-do list, not my own.*

March 13

But do people know where to find wisdom?
Where can they find understanding?
~Job 28:12

True wisdom and understanding are not found among the living here on Earth. Fearing God is the beginning of knowledge and wisdom. God is a generous giver and will bless you with true, pure wisdom when you ask.

When you're faced with the next big decision, depart from your typical path of browsing google, picking up another book, or going to a friend for advice. For true wisdom and discernment, talk to your Sovereign Lord.

Dear Father,

Your wisdom is magnificent. Your exceptional details, brilliant knowledge, creative resourcefulness, and amazing foresight astound me! Please grant me discernment and bless me with Your wisdom so that I know I'm making the right decisions today.

March 14

You can be sure of this: The Lord set apart the godly for himself. The Lord will answer when I call to him.
~Psalms 4:3

There's no reason to be skeptical about this. Children of God are *set apart*. He hears everything you pray and <u>will answer you</u>.

It's your job to make sure that your eyes have clear visibility. It's up to you to make sure your ears are receptive to the Holy Spirit's voice. You are free to talk to the Lord about anything that is on your mind.

Dear Lord,

Thank you for setting me apart as Your special treasure. Please make your answers known to me in a way I can understand. Give me the joy to accept whatever your answer is and the courage to obey all of Your instructions.

March 15

No wonder my heart is glad, and I rejoice.
My body rests in safety!
~Psalms 16:9

Natural disasters, horrible crimes, fires, transportation accidents, and terminal illnesses are all present in our fallen world.

Despite <u>whatever danger you're in the middle of</u>, you can rejoice and be glad because *God is with you* and nothing can deter His protection. You won't find such a refuge anywhere on earth! Place your hope and trust in Jesus – the unsurpassable security guard.

Dear God,

I praise your mighty name! Thank you for protecting me from both the visible and the unseen evil forces that surround me. When I am afraid in the danger, please give me Your absolute peace, reassuring me that everything is okay since You are with me.

March 16

*God's way is perfect. All the Lord's promises prove true. He is
a shield for all who look to him for protection.*
~Psalms 18:30

We strive to be impeccable, better than others. We constantly
look for the perfect home, the perfect spouse, the perfect job,
the perfect cure, or the perfect answers…. stop searching.

God is perfection. Seek Him FIRST and above all, and then, all
of the intricate details of your life, including your hopes for
your desires, will fall right into place. You'll be blessed
beyond belief.

Dear Jesus,

*Replace the desire within me to always have the "perfect" things
with a burning desire to seek You. I know that You are perfection
and that You promise to work every detail, every situation, every
struggle, and every painful ache into Your will. Thank you for all
the blessings You've already given me as well as all the future
blessings.*

March 17

Show me the right path, O Lord;
point out the road for me to follow.
~Psalms 25:4

We are faced with hundreds of decisions and multiple paths to take every day. How do you know which way to go? Never go one way based solely on your own feelings or what other people are pushing you towards. It's crucial to ask God which way He wants you to travel.

Sometimes He provides a smooth, easy road to journey on and other times, the road God leads you to includes speed bumps requiring you to slow down, challenges to overcome, and/or detours to take. Straying from your protective shepherd can lead you towards a destructive, dangerous, and/or more frightening path. <u>His road is the best one to take.</u> Even if there are dangers and challenges on His road, rest assured because <u>if He led you to it, He will get you through it.</u>

Dear God,

Please clearly show me the right road to take. I know that wherever You lead me, that is where You want me. Please give me courage to go on unknown paths and those that include my fears, worries, and insecurities. Thank you for being my faithful, loving shepherd. I trust You and Your paths.

March 18

The Lord is my light and my salvation, so why should I be afraid? The Lord is my fortress, protecting me from danger, so why should I tremble?
~Psalms 27:1

The enemy can form weapons against you, but none of them will prosper when God's Holy Spirit resides within you!

The Holy Spirit is what empowers you. The enemy will stumble and all of his schemes will fail when he comes across the Holy Spirit within you. Be brave and confident in all of your battles because God is your extraordinary safeguard.

Dear Lord,

Help me to face my fears boldly and to fight by faith not sight. Help me rely on the Holy Spirit and Your strength rather than my own abilities. You are my rock, my fortress, and my shield!

March 19

The lord says, "I will guide you along the best pathway for your life. I will advise you and watch over you."
~Psalms 32:8

You have free will. You can choose whatever path you want to take. You can choose your friends, what you do in your free time, and where you live and work. But, if you want the absolute best, unparalleled life you can live, then follow Jesus Christ, <u>listening to Him</u> and <u>going where He leads</u>.

Our revered Father never takes his eyes off you. He knows where you are every second of every day. If the Lord brings you to a mountain, then He will help you overcome it! Don't worry.

Dear Jesus,

I commit to following you! Thank you for being my Savior and guiding me on the path of abundant life. Whenever I wander from Your path, bring me back quickly.

March 20

But the lord's plans stand firm forever;
his intentions can never be shaken.
~Psalms 33:11

You can try to change people or circumstances in your life, and they may temporarily change, but God's ultimate plan always prevails. He does not change and neither will His plan for the world.

People change their minds all the time. Your boss or coworkers may reverse a decision that was previously in your favor. Your loved ones may disappoint you or walk out on you when circumstances become stressful or painful. Your friends may forsake you.

God is the opposite. His faithfulness endures forever, regardless of the situation you're in. His mercy overflows unto you, regardless of how you act. He is always gracious and forgiving, no matter what you've done. His unconditional love is relentless and never-ending.

Dear Father,

I am so grateful that I can always rely on you without a shadow of a doubt. I never have to worry if Your character will change or if You will not follow through on a promise just because things are difficult. Thank you for your pure faithfulness, amazing mercy, beautiful grace, constant forgiveness, and endless love.

March 21

The lord is close to the brokenhearted; he rescues those whose spirits are crushed. The righteous person faces many troubles, but the lord comes to rescue each time.
~Psalms 34:18

If your heart is torn, your body crumbled, or your mind afflicted, then you should be glad that your Rescuer is coming!

He is ever so close to you when your spirit is crushed. So, although you feel like you're drowning, be encouraged because Jesus is right at your side extending His compassion and comfort unto you, and sending his peace into your soul. Praise Him always.

Dear Jesus,

My spirit is crushed and I feel as though I cannot go on. Breathe joy into my heart again. Send both energy and strength to my muscles and bones again. Infuse peace into my anxious, tangled mind. I need you every moment of every day. Jesus, even though I feel completely defeated and broken, I thank you for this time because it is another opportunity to trust you and to feel your loving presence.

March 22

Though they stumble, they will never fall,
for the lord holds them by the hand.
~Psalms 37:24

This is directed towards "godly" people. Even though we face everything from minor difficulties to severe tragedies, we will never be defeated because God, who's already won, is holding our hand every step of the way!

Losing balance, falling down, and making mistakes are all inevitable. This is how we learn. As children of the Almighty King, we do not have to worry or become angered when we mess up because He keeps us from falling down permanently.

Dear God,

The next time I trip, I will cling to your steady hand. Thank you for continuously holding me up and keeping me secure in Your loving arms. When I stumble, teach me what You want me to learn and help me to get right back on track.

March 23

Then, call on me when you're in trouble, and I'll rescue you, and you'll give me the glory!
~Psalms 50:15

When disorder or misfortune burst into your life, call on Jesus. First of all, He will rescue you. Once you recognize Jesus is the One who got you through that difficulty, you give praise and honor to His Father. Jesus doesn't save you just for your sake. He saves you so that *God will be glorified.*

Many people around us see an impossible situation or deep wound that can't be recovered from, but when they see you praising Jesus for helping you, they will be more likely to give glory to God the next time they're in such a predicament.

Dear God,

I am stuck and need your help. Rescue me from my burdens and troubles. Help me be a light to others who lack faith so that Your presence shines and encourages them. To God be the glory!

March 24

*Give your burdens to the lord, and he'll take care of you. He
will not permit the godly to slip and fall!*
~Psalms 55:22

We are weighed down with a plethora of feelings, thoughts,
and tasks every day. The good news is that we are not meant
to carry all those burdens. God can hold the weight of the
entire world upon His shoulders without wavering or
collapsing. He will accept any and all burdens whenever you
surrender them to Him.

Dear God,

*I am tired and weary. My mind is overwhelmed with all I need to do
each day. I am stressed and anxious. Lord, I need You. Please take
away all the deadweight and excess baggage that is taking up
residence in my mind and heart.*

March 25

Your unfailing love is better than life itself; how I praise you!
~Psalms 63:3

We're "flying high" when everything in our lives goes how
we want and when everyone we love is doing well. We are
enthusiastic, passionate, and awakened when we receive our
desires. Think of how elated you felt during the happiest time
in your life.

<u>God's unfailing love is better than all of your happiest</u>
<u>moments put together</u>. His love is indescribable. Even when
we sin or turn from him, He loves us the same. Praise Him
forever!

Dear God,

Your constant love floods into my soul even when I sin and mess up.
I cannot praise you enough! Thank you for loving me
unconditionally. Thank you for your endless grace, forgiveness, and
mercy.

March 26

Summon your might, O God. Display your power, O God,
as you have in the past.
~Psalms 68:28

It's crucial to always remember and reflect on the track record
you have with God. Think of all the times He has proven His
faithfulness. Reflect on all the times He has been gracious to
you. Reminisce on all the times you have seen His
unbelievable miracles performed and incredible power
demonstrated.

Dear God,

You helped me in the past so I know You can do it again. Holy
Spirit, allow my eyes to see beyond the ordinary and into the
phenomenal ways You are working.

March 27

He changes rivers into deserts, and springs of water
into dry, thirsty land.
~Psalms 107:33

There is no other like the Lord! He is simply tremendous! His miracles are limitless. He is working within you to build your character, strengthen your faith, and infuse a desire for His will.

Plus, God is working *through you*. When others see you respond to challenges or tragedies with thanksgiving and praise, they are getting a glimpse of Jesus' light. Yes, God is continuously working on your character, but He may also have others on His agenda. Sometimes, the Lord builds someone else's faith or sharpens his/her character *through you*.

Just as God can literally transform a river into a desert and a spring of water into dry land, He can cure your "irreparable" disease. He can heal your deepest heartache. He can solve your "impossible" problem. He can do the unthinkable!

Dear God,

There is none like You! I surrender my heart, mind, and soul to you. I want to be your vessel on earth, helping others come to know You, so I accept how You choose to work within and through me.

March 28

Open my eyes to see the wonderful truths in your instructions.
~Psalms 119:18

Many of us do try to seek God daily. We go to church to learn from our amazing pastors, praise Him through wonderful worship songs, participate in great Bible studies, and are involved with various life groups. What good is all that if we don't see or understand the truths God is teaching us through His Word?

Rather than simply reading the Bible or singing worship songs routinely, *think about the words*. What are you learning about God's character? What is He trying to teach you?

Dear God,

As I read your word, point out the truths You want me to learn. Help me to learn quickly and apply Your instructions immediately. Give me a heavenly perspective so I can see the value in Your instructions.

March 29

Point out anything in me that offends you, and lead me along
the path of everlasting life.
~Psalms 139:24

Committing to following Jesus is not just a statement you tell others. It requires you to leave your personal path or the way of others and instead run confidently to His path. It requires you to not only allow Him to point out your sin, faults, and offenses, but to be ready to repent so you can realign yourself to the path of righteousness and everlasting life.

Dear Jesus,

I recognize that you are the only way to an abundant, blessed, joyful life. I give up going my own way and instead choose to follow your path! I invite you to chisel away all of my negative thoughts, poor attitudes, and negative traits that don't align with Your word. Thank you for making me a better person and for leading me along the path of eternal life!

March 30

Teach me to do your will, for you are my God. May your gracious Spirit lead me forward on a firm footing.
~Psalms 143:10

We all make plans. Some of us are quite determined "go getters," never ceasing to do whatever it takes to make sure the plan is intact and done accurately. We are bothered or grow anxious when our plan doesn't work out or yield the results we want. Others make plans, but are inconsistent with following through and may not mind at all if the plan fails. Then, there are those who do not plan ahead.

Everyone has some kind of plan/goal about one thing or the other, whether it be in their personal or professional life.

Time and time again the Bible reminds us to surrender our plans to God. Following personal plans while ignoring God's will can lead to stumbling. When you know that you are following His plan, you can have complete peace and confidence. The Holy Spirit will guide you "forward on a firm footing."

Dear God,

I relinquish every plan I have to You. Show me what Your plan is for my life and help me follow it with enthusiasm, boldness, and joy! Thank you for guiding me forward and keeping me stable.

March 31

No one enjoys being wrongly accused, mistreated, or judged unfairly. And yet, we often treat others this way, especially when someone attacks us first. We tend to retaliate and/or gossip. Both our actions and words are incredibly powerful, doing significantly more damage than we realize. <u>Thinking</u> negatively about others is a sneaky sin. Jesus tells us to *love our enemies and pray for those who persecute us.*

Not only do we mistreat others, but we disobey God as well. Even though we sin, He remains compassionate towards us. He always forgives. His grace and mercy are anew each morning.

Dear God,

Thank you for giving me grace and for showering your endless compassion upon me even when I sin. Father, help me extend patience and grace to others. Help me quickly forgive my persecutors. Help me to be good to everyone.

April 1

Cry out for insight, and ask for understanding.
~Proverbs 2:3

It is not enough to simply ask your heavenly Father for insight, advice, or guidance. What do you do upon receiving that information? We must ask for <u>understanding</u> as well. The Holy Spirit, which already lives within us, is what whispers truth and guides us to the right choices.

A mechanic can know what an engine, car battery, fuel pump, and other parts look like and know where they belong under the hood, but he is useless if he doesn't <u>understand</u> how they work. Similarly, we can memorize Bible verses, recite the books of the Bible in order, and know details about the people in the Bible, but what good is that if we do not <u>understand</u> God's Word?

Dear God,

Help me understand Your Truth so I can live out Your will better. I do not simply want to know what the Bible says. Father, I need a genuine understanding about You and Your Truth to help me live out Your will here on earth.

April 2

Trust in the lord with all your heart;
do not depend on your own understanding.
~Proverbs 3:5

From small, seemingly insignificant tasks and choices to large, seemingly unsurmountable ones, put all of your trust in God. His plan is flawless.

More often than not, you won't understand because God's mysterious ways are typically not comprehendible for our finite minds. So, relax. You won't understand, and that is okay. You can and should still obey because He is God.

If He is convicting you to do something, talk to or forgive someone, or go somewhere, then simply obey, and do so <u>without doubt or fear</u>. Trust Jesus. Wait in hopeful anticipation to see the blessings come to fruition.

Dear Lord,

Give me the strength to let go of my understanding and latch onto faith instead. Make me aware of whatever is holding me back from fully trusting you and help me to get rid of it. Please give me a heavenly perspective and a relaxed state of mind so my anxiety can melt away. Lord, I will obey even when I don't understand.

April 3

My child, do not reject the lord's discipline, and
don't be upset when he corrects you.
~Proverbs 3:11

Discipline can feel like punishment. Understand that God never chastises you because of your sin and that when He disciplines, it is always out of love.

He may discipline to teach you a lesson, draw you closer to Him, or to remind you of your dependency on Him. Furthermore, He may discipline you in order to draw someone else to Him. Ultimately, He is glorified.

Don't reject when the Lord corrects you. Replace your negativity and anger with positivity, joy, and <u>thankfulness.</u> Open your mind to *see* what He is trying to show or instruct you!

Remember, God uses everything for good! You may not notice right away *why* you went through that situation, but eventually, whether here on earth after your spiritual ears and eyes have been opened more, or later when you're in heaven, you will.

Dear God,

Thank you for your correction. I know your intentions are pure and good! Help me to not merely just accept your discipline, but to be joyful and grateful for it.

April 4

Pride leads to disgrace, but with humility comes wisdom.
~Proverbs 11:2

Have you ever heard the saying, "Knowledge is power?" If you strive to be knowledgeable, in any area of your life, humble yourself.

Don't brag about what you know. Learn from your mistakes instead of growing angry, bitter, or frustrated when you stumble or fail. Soak in constructive criticism like a sponge instead of becoming defensive or offensive. Wisdom comes when you are humble and teachable.

Jesus is the perfect picture of humility, and He had His father's wisdom because of that.

Dear Jesus,

I invite you into my soul to humble my heart. Show me every area in my life where I am selfish, greedy, and prideful. Keep me humble when I'm blessed with success and prosperity. Jesus, infuse a teachable attitude into my mind. Keep my eyes fixed on Your humble, loving heart.

April 5

Wealth from get-rich-quick schemes quickly disappears;
wealth from hard work grows over time.
~Proverbs 11:12

Rushing into an opportunity or project often leads to a downfall. Satisfying desires of the flesh with immediate "cures" result in the "need" for more soon after. Don't try cutting corners to reach an outcome or destination faster. Prosperity and wealth grow with hard work done over time.

If you're not prospering right now, yet you're working hard, then just be patient. Your wealth and blessings are <u>growing while you work!</u> During this season of waiting, gaze upon the Lord, communicate with Him, and remain steady in your faith. Persevere. Endure. Stick it out. Your time will come.

Dear Lord,

Help me to resist the desire for immediate results. Help me start strong and remain determined to push forward when I am in a season of waiting. Father, I need your strength. Please bless me with endurance to stay the course.

April 6

People who despise advice are asking for trouble; those who respect a command will succeed.
~Proverbs 11:13

This says it all. Release your pride. Let go of your anger when someone provides constructive criticism. Disengage your excuses when given a task you don't want to do. Rather, <u>accept and respect</u> criticism, instruction, and demands.

Some of us simply don't seek advice enough because we believe we can solve the problem ourselves. Some of us seek guidance, but certainly don't respond in a way God prefers.

Trouble will arise whenever you disregard advice, and success will emerge whenever you respect and take advice.

Dear Father,

Point out to me the decisions I should seek guidance on. Replace any feelings of anger and pride with joy and humility instead. Jesus, thank you for being my example and leading me on the path of righteousness.

April 7

Gentle words are a tree of life;
a deceitful tongue crushes the spirit.
~Proverbs 15:4

Graceless and malicious words can sabotage relationships, shatter hearts, and abuse spirits. Considerate and sympathetic words can blossom relationships, prosper hearts, and purify spirits.

Do your words give life or death? Choose your words carefully and precisely.

Dear Jesus,

Thank you for always speaking kindly and tenderly to me. Jesus, I want Your gentleness to be expressed through my words. Please soften my tone of voice, especially in times when I am flustered or upset.

April 8

You can make many plans, but the lord's purpose will prevail!
~Proverbs 19:21

Sure, we can organize awesome events, map out what we feel is an excellent path, and create a top-notch schedule that is sure to work beautifully. Sometimes our plan works how we intended it to and in our favor, and sometimes it just doesn't. We implement the plan, but it fails. The plan is changed or ruined before it even begins. God's plan will always come out on top. He does whatever is necessary to ensure His plan materializes.

So, if your plan changes, doesn't work, or is destroyed, *relax and thank God.* How can you thank Him when your flawless plan didn't work? You can thank Him because He is all-knowing and His plans are to prosper you, whether you feel it or not. A thankful attitude toward your Father brings more blessings than you'll ever realize.

Dear God,

When my plan doesn't work how I thought it would, I will praise You anyway! I know You are in control. When my plan fails or is destroyed, I will thank You anyway! Teach me what You want me to learn. When my plan completely changes, I will be grateful to You anyway! Your ways are always best for me. My greatest desire is to follow Your plans. Please help me surrender my agendas and ideas, and to follow Yours.

April 9

The lord directs our steps, so why try to understand
everything along the way?
~Proverbs 20:24

This verse is so encouraging! We can let go of over-analyzing our problems and trying to solve them. We don't have to try so hard to understand why things happen. Remember that God is the chief executive officer of our lives who will direct our steps.

Follow Him and you don't *need to understand* because when You're with God, you know you're exactly where He intends you to be. Relax and follow where He leads. There's absolutely no reason to question Him or analyze His instructions/direction.

Dear Lord,

Thank you for directing my path each and every day. I am tired of trying to understand everything. I place my trust in You even when I don't know all the details.

April 10

People may be right in their own eyes,
but the lord examines their heart.
~Proverbs 21:2

God continuously scans your heart. He thoroughly inspects it, looking for the beauty within. He knows every thorn that is keeping you from the fulfilled life He has for you.

We all sin. God's marvelous love for us is so deep that He sent Jesus to die on the cross *for us*. When you accept Jesus as your Savior and invite him into your heart, He removes the thorns and cleanses you from all sin. Your heart is made new.

Confess your sins and repent. God knows when your heart is genuine.

Dear God,

Thank you for sending Your one and only son to die for my sins. I am sorry for all of my sins. I repent and turn to You right now. I invite You into my heart to analyze it. Do whatever is necessary to remove the thorns from my heart! Father, purify my heart again, making it new.

April 11

Good planning and hard work lead to prosperity, but hasty shortcuts lead to poverty.
~Proverbs 21:5

We crave instant gratification. We dash into relationships, race to buy that "perfect" house or car, run to an addiction to feel better fast, and expedite projects to reach the end result quickly.

Our impatience and hurried lifestyle lead to shortcuts that may provide a sense of <u>temporary gladness</u>, but ultimately that joy will fade away. Success and prosperity come from following Jesus on His path. Remember, hurry is not God's nature, so stay away from "shortcuts."

Set a plan in place, but remain flexible because God has the authority to adapt it at any moment. Work hard and persevere. Most importantly, <u>be patient while trusting God.</u>

Dear God,

I am sorry for taking shortcuts, straying off Your path. I know that although Your way can take longer than I wish, include obstacles I don't want to deal with, and/or fears that I don't want to face, it is the best way. Grant me the strength to refuse shortcuts and endurance to push on when challenges arise.

April 12

*The wise are mightier than the strong, and those with
knowledge grow stronger and stronger.*
~Proverbs 24:5

Having knowledge and experience is more beneficial than
physical strength. When faced with a difficult decision, seek
support from others who have been in your shoes. When
struggling in a relationship, seek guidance from Godly
mentors who are in healthy relationships. When you are
depressed, overwhelmed, or afraid, seek encouragement and
support from someone who can help.

Seek the Lord first, asking Him who you should turn to for
support and advice. God didn't intend for us to go through
life alone.

Dear Father,

*I want to grow in wisdom. Please give me an understanding heart
and mind. Bless me with the gift of discernment. Pour an eagerness
to learn and grow into my soul! Help me realize when I need to seek
help from others, and make me brave enough to do so.*

April 13

Don't rejoice when your enemies fall;
don't be happy when they stumble.
~Proverbs 24:17

Jesus Christ came to heal and help us. He never clapped when sinful people slipped or collapsed. Full of compassion, He helped them back up. Pray for those who hurt you and help them if they fall. Blessings will certainly follow such a loving response.

Dear Jesus,

Teach me how to be more compassionate and empathetic, especially to those who mistreat me. Help me to want to lend them a hand when they need one. Keep my heart pure and kind.

April 14

People who conceal their sins will not prosper, but if they confess and turn from them, they'll receive mercy.
~Proverbs 28:13

Your heavenly Father <u>already knows</u> every sinful thought, word, and action you've done. He knows your sin before you even commit it. There is no point in hiding it because the Lord sees clearly through any covering you attempt. It's useless to run from it. It's also meaningless to ignore it.

All He wants you to do is be mindful of your sin, confess it verbally, and, with a genuine heart and desire to repent, ask Him for forgiveness. When you repent and turn back to Him, you *will* receive His endless mercy no matter how dark or deep your sin and no matter how many times in the past you've committed that sin.

Dear God,

I am sorry for trying to hide my sin from You, others, and myself. Help me face it and repent! I am sorry for running away from it. Lord, help me run towards it instead and to gratefully receive Your mercy. I am sorry for ignoring it. Help me embrace it and move forward in Your grace and forgiveness. Thank you for continuously showering me with mercy.

April 15

For everything, there's a season,
a time for every activity under heaven.
~Ecclesiastes 3:1

Don't dwell on the past, hoping things were as they used to be. Don't fantasize so much about the future, wishing that certain things will take place. The past has already come and gone.

The future belongs to the Lord. Live in the present moment, taking note of all that God is already doing in your life! The spouse, child, career, home, healing, solution to a major problem, or breakthrough you're desiring **will come**, but it will come *after you place total trust in God and His timing* and when you *surrender yourself to His will.* It will come in His timing, so you must be patient and not lose faith!

We go through different seasons of life, and God works everything in that season, whether we realize it or not, into His mystifying, yet beautiful design.

Dear Lord,

Keep me in the present with You. Please help me to stop dwelling on my past – previous trials, mistakes, sin, and pain. Oh Father, please immediately erase any worry about the future that comes up. I know You are with me in the very present, which is where I receive Your tranquil peace.

April 16

Enjoy what you have rather than desiring what you don't
have. Just dreaming about nice things is meaningless –
like chasing the wind.
~Ecclesiastes 6:9

Even if you only have the clothes on your back, be thankful
and praise God. Wishing for beautiful clothes, lavish cars, and
fancy homes is like "chasing the wind" because these earthly
possessions are temporary! Furthermore, they are just <u>things!</u>
These things are meaningless because your true home is
heaven.

Thanking and praising the Lord continuously, regardless of
what you "have" here, will allow Him to store up astonishing
treasures for you in heaven. Heavenly treasures are what you
should be striving for since these rewards can never fade
away!

Dear Father,

Please make my heart more appreciative of the things I do have. Bless
me with a thankful mindset. Take away the desire to want useless
things and grant me a deep passion to desire what You find good,
pure, loving, and kind.

April 17

Accept the way God does things,
for who can straighten what he has made crooked?
~Ecclesiastes 7:13

It is simply impossible to adjust anything that God has made or caused to happen. Accept the Lord's ways! He is our Master of all creation, in full control of the entire world and everything in it. It's ridiculous to even attempt at straightening or bending something He crafted.

Stop trying to analyze why or how He works. Discontinue trying to make things go your way, no matter how good your intentions are. *Accept* how He works so you can be free from stress, anxiety, and worry. *Thank Him* for how He works, even when it is unfair, frightening, and/or painful. Rest in the truth that He works everything into His pattern for good for those who love Him.

Dear Lord,

I am sorry for trying to change the ways You are working. I surrender fully to you. Help me to relax when I am afraid and lean on Your love when I am hurting. Father, I want to let go of control and wholeheartedly accept all of Your ways in my life, so please help me in this area. Do whatever you need to do within my soul so that I can rely on You without any doubt or fear.

April 18

People can never predict when hard times might come.
Like fish in a net or birds in a trap,
people are caught by sudden tragedy.
~Ecclesiastes 9:12

This is why it's crucial to always have God's armor **on**: the belt of truth, breastplate of righteousness, shield of faith, shoes of peace, helmet of salvation, and sword of the spirit!

We are reminded here that trouble and tragedy will strike us, but He promises that He will be right there with us.

You *already have* the armor to fight the good fight. Are you prepared for battle? Or, is your armor set aside collecting dust?

Dear Jesus,

Thank you for keeping me balanced with your Truth. Thank you for the breastplate of righteousness which protects my heart and Your indestructible shield that preserves my faith! Thank you for providing shoes of peace as I walk through the battle and for your shatterproof helmet which covers my salvation. Thank you for the solid, unbreakable sword of the Holy Spirit - the Bible. Jesus, remind me to dress in God's armor daily so that I am prepared for Satan's tactics!

April 19

Many waters cannot quench love, nor can rivers drown it.
If a man tried to buy love with all his wealth,
his offer would be utterly scorned.
~Song of Songs 8:7

Sometimes we try everything to refresh love or push it away.
Other times, we try to buy love through our words or actions.
Love cannot be bought.

God's love cannot be extinguished for He is love! Keep your
focus on Jesus. Pray continuously. His love for you is
unending and unconditional.

Dear God,

Oh how I praise You for Your infinite love. I invite You into my soul
to transform my heart. Help me to love people as You do.

April 20

It will happen as I have planned. It will be as I have decided.
~Isaiah 14:24

The prophet Isiah reminded the people here that the Lord of Heaven's Armies promised to judge Assyria. No nation can resist or eliminate God's plans.

When God shows you the way and tells you His plan, obey and trust! His plan will always transpire regardless of what *you* attempt to do to alter it, so it's better to follow Him in the first place, even if it seems impossible.

Dear God,

Thank you for being in total control at all times. Help me to simply confidently and gladly follow Your plan even when I don't understand or am frightened. I trust you Father!

April 21

The lord of heaven's armies says, "The time will come when I'll pull out the nail that seemed so firm. It will come out and fall to the ground. Everything it supports will fall with it. I, the lord, have spoken!"
~Isaiah 22:25

Do you feel like there's a nail penetrating within you somewhere, fixed in your heart or cemented in your mind, in which you can't remove? This nail causes pain, fear, stress, nervousness, shame, and/or guilt. Your current circumstance appears impossible to overcome. You feel utterly stuck.

These times are certainly uncomfortable, but remember that God is testing and growing your faith, while drawing you closer to Him and reminding you of your dependency on Him. You are insufficient. You need Jesus every moment of every day.

Take your eyes off the current situation and look to your miraculous Father! Praise Him in spite of what you're feeling because there will be a moment, His moment, when He instantly removes that nail. Plus, all negative feelings associated with it will crumble as well! He will free you, enabling you to be at peace once again!

Dear Lord,

This nail within is so painful and I cannot remove it. I need You. Help me to learn what You are teaching me through this experience. Holy Spirit, direct my gaze to God and His love rather than this nail.

April 22

So, the lord must wait for you to come to him so he can show
you his love and compassion. For the lord is a faithful God.
Blessed are those who wait for his help.
~Isaiah 30:18

Admit it when you're wrong. Admit it when you're lost.
Admit it when you're confused. Admit it when you're afraid.
God is waiting for you to communicate with Him. Even
though He already knows your thoughts and how you're
feeling, He wants more than anything for you to decide to go
to Him.

He overflows with compassion. Blessings come when you run
to Him with your troubles, burdens, and requests instead of
relying on other people or giving into your flesh's desires.

Dear God,

Thank you for waiting for me! I am so sorry for ignoring you. I am
sorry for choosing to seek others or my own desires rather than your
council first. I am sorry for rushing into things when you tell me to
wait upon you. Thank you for your faithful love showering me with
endless compassion whenever I come to you!

April 23

Have you never heard? Have you never understood?
The Lord is the everlasting God, the Creator of all the earth.
He never grows weak or weary.
No one can measure the depths of his understanding.
~Isaiah 40:28

The Lord has no equal. He is supreme above all creation. Everything on heaven and earth is created by Him and for His glory. Although we are weak, we can rejoice because His strength and power never run low. Exhaustion may take its toll on us, but the Lord never becomes fatigued. When you are disheartened, praise the Lord because you don't need to rely on your strength in that moment. Rely on God! He will get you through to the other side. He will reenergize you and refuel your faith so that you can keep going.

We often do not understand why we go through such harsh trials, pain, or heartache. His ways are incomprehensible. *We can still rest* knowing that He is for us and wants what's best for us. He sees the whole picture. Let go and let God work. Surrender to the ways He works in your life.

Dear Heavenly Father,

I submit fully to you, especially in times of hardship. I trust that You are working it out for good because that is Your promise. Lord, help me to let go of wanting to understand. Help me release the desire to want to know every detail. Instead, I want to fully trust in the ways in which You are working in my life, my loved ones' lives, my community, and the world.

April 24

*But those who trust in the lord will find new strength. They'll
soar high on wings like eagles. They'll run and not grow
weary. They'll walk and not faint.*
~Isaiah 40:31

If you are weakened physically by a sickness or disease, you
can still find strength and hope. If you are bruised
emotionally, you can still find joy. If you are broken
spiritually, you can find complete healing. When you realize
that trusting God is the way to live, His strength, hope, joy,
and healing will take residence within your needy soul.

Trusting in God doesn't only render strength. Prosperity and
blessings follow as well. You will continue moving forward
without becoming tired, weary, frightened, or worried. You
will walk confidently because your trust is not in yourself,
others, or what you see, but rather it is in your Mighty Savior!

Dear Lord,

*When I feel like I just can't go on, You are the One who always gets
me through. You are the One who re-energizes me, renews my
strength, refreshes my hope, and restores my faith. I trust you.*

April 25

God says, "At just the right time, I'll respond to you."
~Isaiah 49:8

We crave instant gratification and immediate solutions to our problems. The Lord often uses delays to test our faith and grow our patience.

How many times do you find yourself praying, "Please hurry Lord. Take this pain away. Fix this problem. Help me right now."

We must remember to *relax* and that His timing is always best. We cannot rush God. He will respond *at just the right time.* Taking short cuts and rushing will likely delay the blessing. Relax and wait on the One who is in control.

Be *persistent* in prayer. Be *patient* while waiting for God's answer. Be *prepared* to give Him the glory!

Dear God,

Although waiting is difficult, I know Your timeline is perfect. Give me patience and comfort as I wait for Your response. Please help me refrain from rushing. Keep my faith and hope in You steady and sure.

April 26

"My thoughts are nothing like your thoughts," says the lord.
"And my ways are far beyond anything you could imagine."
~Isaiah 55:8

We pray for what we want or think is best for either ourselves, our family and friends, or the world in general. Our mere minds can't think of anything that come anywhere close to God's ingenious ideas.

When you submit to His will, obey Him fully, and trust that He will work everything out for good, not only will you reap blessings, but those blessings will be beyond your wildest imagination!

Dear Lord,

I praise your glorious name! I realize that I will never fully comprehend Your ways because You are the Almighty Lord most high! Help me to release the desire to understand everything and instead, strengthen my trust in You.

April 27

They'll fight you, but they'll fail.
For I am with you, and I'll take care of you.
~Jeremiah 1:19

There will be times when people attack you verbally and/or physically. When you are grounded in the fact that your incredible, all-powerful Lord is always with you and <u>when you trust</u> that He will get you through, you will be comforted and at peace instead of fearful and weak.

Dear Lord,

When enemies approach, I will cling to Your promise "I am with you." When I'm in a battle, I will hold onto Your promise "I'll take care of you." Thank you for your security and comfort.

April 28

Can anyone hide from me in a secret place?
Am I not everywhere in all the heavens and earth?
~Jeremiah 23:24

It's foolish and irresponsible to even think of hiding from the Lord. He is omnipresent.

You have a choice to make: run away from Him and hide from your troubles or run towards Him embracing your trials. He is right at your fingertips, ready and fully equipped to help.

Dear Heavenly Father,

I am sorry for trying to hide my feelings, hide from my problem, and hide from You. Help me to run both boldly and joyfully to You when I'm hurting, lost, confused, frightened, or facing challenges. I know that You can and will help me through when I place my trust in You. So right now Father, I fully surrender to You and place my full trust in Your strength.

April 29

For I know the plans I have for you. They are plans for good and not for disaster, to give you a future and a hope.
~Jeremiah 29:11

Whatever storm you are in the midst of right now, do not be discouraged. Depression, worry, and fear come ever so easily when you only look at what's right in front of you during the storm. Faith requires endurance. When you feel as though you're drowning and there's no hope, cling to Jesus.

There is purpose in the storm! Not a single tear is wasted. God is mysteriously working all sorrow and hardships into His good design. His tender, loyal heart is devoted to you. His plans are for you to thrive.

Dear God,

Thank you for reminding me that You are for me. When I am full of despair, I ask that you replenish my hope. Give me the courage to embrace the storms of my life. Grant me a heavenly perspective during my hardships. I pray that nothing and no one blocks me from seeing Your Truth or diminshes my faith.

April 30

I say to myself, "The lord is my inheritance;
therefore, I'll hope in him!"
~Lamentations 3:24

God cannot fail you! It's ridiculous to place <u>all</u> of your hope in any one person, no matter how much you love or trust them. The only One you should place all of your hope, faith, and complete trust in is Jesus Christ – your inheritance!

Dear Jesus,

Because of your death on the cross, I have an eternal inheritance. How can I ever thank you enough? Jesus, my Savior, you are my hope. I will follow You, trusting where You lead and obeying Your instructions.

May 1

Son of man, let all my words sink deep into your own heart first. Listen to them carefully for yourself.
~Ezekiel 3:10

Ezekiel saw the glory of the Lord – the figure of a man with a glowing halo all around him, shining in brilliant splendor. The Spirit went into him and spoke, and Ezekiel listened carefully.

Pay attention to the words *let* and *sink deep*. The Holy Spirit asks us to let His words to flow within us without fighting back.

Submit your mind to the Lord and listen so that other voices clamoring for your attention don't win. God doesn't ask you to solely listen to His message. He wants the words to penetrate deep into your heart, and for you to apply His instructions in your daily life.

Dear Father,

Make me sensitive to the Holy Spirit's voice and enable me to not merely hear the words, but to allow them to saturate both my heart and mind. Please help me to obey the voice of Truth without worry or resistance.

May 2

Those who are wise will shine as bright as the sky, and those who lead many to righteousness will shine like stars forever.
~Daniel 12:3

As Christians, it should be a priority of ours to lead as many people as possible to salvation through Jesus Christ. We are called to teach the Good News: God sent His only Son Jesus Christ to die on the cross for our lives.

Jesus purifies us from our sins so that we may have eternal life in heaven. All those who confess with their mouth and believe in their heart that Jesus is their Savior are saved by grace and will spend eternity in heaven.

Lead others to the path of righteousness, the path of LIFE – Jesus Christ.

Dear Jesus,

Thank you for giving up your life so that I could live in eternity with you and our Father. Thank you for cleansing me of all sin and constantly forgiving me. Thank you for your unending and compassionate love! Thank you for guiding me along the path of righteousness and life.

May 3

Oh that we might know the lord! Let us press on to know him. He'll respond to us as surely as the arrival of dawn or the coming of rains in early spring.
~Hosea 6:3

You know with certainty that the sun will rise every morning, and not only that, but you expect it to. You can be just as confident that God will respond to your prayers! So, wait in expectation. He is always in position.

All He wants is an intimate relationship with you and for you to make Him the center of every area in your life.

Dear Lord,

Ignite a fire within me to want to know you more and more. I want to develop a special and profound relationship with you. Please give me the strength to press on during hard times and the encouragement to be persistent in my prayer requests.

May 4

*Plant the good seeds of righteousness, and you'll harvest a
crop of love. Plow up the hard ground of your hearts, for
now's the time to seek the lord, that he may come and shower
righteousness upon you!*
~Hosea 10:12

Notice the verbs *plant* and *plow*. You have to do the work of
"planting" good seeds of goodness, honor, and love into
others' lives. You have to do the work of "plowing" your
hardened hearts. Eliminate all unnecessary, negative, and
irrational feelings, thoughts, and words that are woven into
your heart. God will certainly help you in both of these areas.

Dear God,

*I invite you into my soul right now. Reveal anything within me that
is hardening my heart. Please help me to do whatever it takes to get
rid of it. I don't want anything to block or ruin seeds of
righteousness. Holy Spirit, teach me how to plant good seeds of
righteousness within myself and others.*

May 5

Don't tear your clothing in your grief, but tear your hearts instead. Return to the lord your God, for he's merciful and compassionate, slow to get angry and filled with unfailing love. He's eager to relent and not punish. ~Joel 2:13

When you've been wronged, troubled, angered, or beaten down, just talk to God about what's on your heart. He is <u>full</u> of mercy and compassion, and is craving to help you.

When we do our part (pray and trust in Him), He will do His (answer and bless).

Dear God,

My heart is shattered. My mind is torn. I am in such deep grief and despair. I come to You in need of Your love, comfort, and peace. Please mend my broken heart. Please give me clarity, wisdom, and discernment about my current situation and decisions that need to be made. Father, please turn my grief, anguish, and sorrow into unexplainable joy. Thank you in advance for healing me. I love you Lord.

May 6

The lion has roared, so who isn't frightened? The sovereign lord has spoken, so who can refuse to proclaim his name?
~Amos 3:8

Jesus doesn't want you to be afraid of Him. "Fearing" the Lord is referring to having a great sense of respect and awe of Him. Furthermore, the "fear" refers to submission to your heavenly Father. Never refuse to profess His everlasting, quintessential, and worthy name.

Dear God,

You are sovereign. I submit to You and choose to follow You wherever You lead. Help me do so with confidence and gladness. I will proclaim Your glorious, mighty name forevermore.

May 7

For the lord is the one who shaped the mountains, stirs up the winds, and reveals his thoughts to mankind. He turns the light of dawn into darkness and treads on the heights of the earth. The lord God of heaven's armies is his name.
~Amos 4:13

Take a few moments to <u>notice and appreciate</u> God's astounding creations. Flowers and plants aren't simply decorations for the yard. They gleam with beauty. Every insect, bird, reptile, fish, and mammal is uniquely made by God. He gave every living creature fascinating qualities and abilities. When hiking up a mountain or taking a long road trip, pay attention to God's magnificent mountains and landforms. Gaze in wonder at His spectacular oceans and stunning waterfalls. Admire the stars and planets in the galaxy.

Our Lord is king of kings, the only one true God. Nothing mankind can ever do, or even imagine, parallels to His marvelous works!

Dear God,

Your creations are astonishing! First, make me more aware of Your exquisite, fascinating, amazing creations and works. Second, instill in me a new and deep appreciation for them. Thank you Father.

May 8

Instead, I want to see a mighty flood of justice,
an endless river of righteous living.
~Amos 5:24

Amos is explaining here that God wants continual, not just seasonal, justice and righteous living. Show fairness at all times and always do your best to live righteously.

"Righteousness" is upright living that aligns with God's expectations. When you know the "right" way to respond or the "right" path to take, you can be confident and brave whenever temptations or attacks approach. The Holy Spirit helps us learn right from wrong.

Dear God,

Thank you for being our perfect, honest, and fair Judge. If I ever start to venture off Jesus' path, please guide my feet back to righteousness immediately. Help me to show justice and live righteously every day, not just in certain seasons.

May 9

*Those who've been rescued will go up to Mount Zion in
Jerusalem to rule over the mountains of Edom,
and the lord himself will be king!*
~Obadiah 1:21

The sovereign Lord revealed the fate of Edom and Israel
through Obadiah. God proclaimed that His people would
ascend to His holy mountain to rule over the mountains of
their ancient foe Edom as a precursor to the coming universal
kingdom. This reminds us that God's children are always
protected, and that we will ascend to be with Him when it's
our time.

Dear God,

*Oh how grateful I am for your uninterrupted, stable, and secure
protection. Thank you for guardian angels who watch over me
through the night and for Your strong hand that keeps evil from
harming me. You are my fortress and I praise Your name!*

May 10

I cried out to the lord in my great trouble,
and he answered me.
~Jonah 2:2

Cry and shout to the Lord during your troubles. Don't sit there passively or nervously talking to Him. Speak up. Pour out all your feelings. He can handle it all - your anger, frustration, sadness, yelling, and bluntness. He is ready and waiting for you to cry out to Him.

He will rescue you! He will either provide an escape route for You to take or pull You right out Himself.

Dear God,

I need You right now more than ever. Please Lord, either show me what Your escape route is so I can be free or send down Your hand for me to grab onto. Jesus, only Your Light can illuminate this terrible darkness I'm in…. reveal it to me! My hope is in You!

May 11

But I'll offer sacrifices to you with songs of praise,
and I'll fulfill all my vows.
For my salvation comes from the lord alone.
~Jonah 2:9

The Lord arranged for a "great fish" to swallow Jonah because he purposely disobeyed God by going in the exact opposite direction of where God clearly told him to go. Jonah was inside the fish for three days and three nights, and then prayed a prayer of deliverance.

Worship is an act of praising Jesus Christ. He smiles ear to ear when His children exalt Him, especially when they praise Him during hard times. No one else saved you like Jesus did – coming to earth as a human and dying for you in spite of all your sin!

Dear Lord,

I give you my songs of praise today! You are worthy of all my attention. Help me to remain completely devoted to You, Father. May no one and nothing distract me from putting You first in all areas of my life.

May 12

When God saw what they had done and how they had put a stop to their evil ways, he changed his mind and did not carry out the destruction he had threatened.
~Jonah 3:10

We all make mistakes. Some of us choose to walk on the wrong path knowing it's harmful. Some of us fail time and time again, through making poor decisions and/or giving into our sinful desires.

No matter how many times we keep going around in that vicious cycle, if we stop our evil ways and repent to our merciful Father, *He will forgive and lovingly embrace us!*

He has an abundant life ready for you. It's better than you could ever imagine. Repent from your sinful ways. Turn to God with all your strength and with a genuine heart.

Dear Father,

I want to live the abundant, blessed life You have for me. I am sorry for not following Your path and for succumbing to my own desires rather than seeking Your will. Please forgive me. Help me to remain grounded in Your truth and determined to always follow You.

May 13

Everyone will live in peace and prosperity, enjoying their own grapevines and fig trees, for there will be nothing to fear. The lord of heaven's armies has made this promise.
~Micah 4:4

The message in the book of Micah is that God's plans for his people will prevail and the nations will come to know Him through his people. Chapter 4, and this verse in particular, focuses on *hope*. Micah reminds the people that they can live without fear because the prosperity and blessings God accomplishes last forever.

If you believe that God is your heavenly Father and that His son Jesus Christ is your personal savior and redeemer, then you have nothing to fear. Peace is readily available to you because God's Holy Spirit abides in you. You can live in peace and prosperity when you place total trust in the Lord.

Dear God,

Your word stands forever. All prosperity comes from You. Thank you for all that You have blessed me with. True peace is found in You. Thank you for making it continuously available to me through your Holy Spirit. Father, when I begin to worry, remind me that because You are with me, I have nothing to fear!

May 14

No, o people, the lord has told you what's good, and this is what he requires of you: to do what's right, to love mercy, and to walk humbly with your God.
~Micah 6:8

He isn't asking us or giving us a choice. He is requiring us to live righteously, love mercy, and walk humbly. Have integrity and make the right choices. Love mercy so that you can forgive others as Jesus forgives you. Walk humbly with Jesus.

Dear Lord,

Show me what I need to change so that I can live righteously. Replace unjust and sinful thoughts and behavior with right and honorable ones. Grant me the blessing of discernment so I can confidently make the right choices. Father, please humble me and help me forgive others as You forgive me.

May 15

As for me, I look to the lord for help. I wait confidently for God to save me, and my God will certainly hear me.
~Micah 7:7

Hopefully the first person you reach out to for help is God. He is your solid foundation fully equipped to handle anything and everything. Not only is He prepared to help you when you call on His name, He yearns to do so.

His love for you is unfathomable. He knows exactly what you need even before you utter a word. He knows exactly how to help you before even doing so. Talk to Him and seek His council. Then, as Micah says here, *wait confidently.*

Dear God,

I know that You will answer my prayer in just the perfect time. Although I don't know when or how You will answer, I will confidently wait upon You. I trust You, Your ways, and Your timing. Thank you for being my security and my loving, faithful Father.

May 16

Don't gloat over me, my enemies! For though I fall, I will rise again. Though I sit in darkness, the lord will be my light.
~Micah 7:8

Regardless of how hard or how many times you fall, do not become unsettled. Get back up. No matter how dark your surroundings are, how frightening your current circumstance is, or how heartbreaking of a tragedy you're struggling with, Jesus is your light! His light is impossible to burn out. In fact, it doesn't even flicker! It shines brilliantly at all times. Seek Jesus with all your soul, and <u>you will find hope</u> in the midst of your trouble. <u>The darkness will fade</u> with His radiant Light.

Dear Jesus,

You are worthy of all praise. Thank you for being my Light in the darkness! Thank you for being my hope when I fall. I know that no matter how dark and frightening my situation may be, Your light still illuminates and is what will guide me out of that darkness. I praise Your glorious name!

May 17

*"Yes," says the Lord, "I will do mighty miracles for you, like
those I did when I rescued you from slavery in Egypt."*
~Micah 7:15

God is the same yesterday, today, and forever! The same God
who gave sight to the blind with His healing hands, caused
the lame to walk with His words, created mankind out of dirt
and His breath, and performed all of the other miracles
witnessed in the Bible is the <u>same living God we serve today</u>!

Expect to see miracles and you will!

Dear God,

*I don't want to miss out on how You are working within me and
around me. Please open up my spiritual eyes so that I can see the
miracles, signs, and wonders You perform each and every day. To
You be the glory, Lord!*

May 18

Once again, you'll have compassion on us.
You'll trample our sins under your feet
and throw them into the depths of the ocean!
~Micah 7:19

There is no one like our God. Because of His unfailing love, He constantly extends grace and compassion, even when we mess up, are broken and weak, or turn away from Him. Moreover, He tramples our sins and fully forgives us! Halleluiah!

Dear Father,

Thank you yet again for Your true, deep compassion that you shower upon me. Thank you for wiping away my sins and endlessly forgiving me. I love you, Father.

May 19

The lord is good, a strong refuge when trouble comes.
He's close to those who trust in him.
~Nahum 1:7

Nahum opens with a poem explaining how our sovereign God will judge the wicked (we are not to judge or seek revenge) and how He is our refuge. We will have trouble in this life, but rely on God's promise "Fear not. I am with you."

Our refuge is the Almighty God of heaven's armies! Trust Him, especially during times of trouble, for He is close to the trustworthy and faithful.

Dear Jesus,

You are my fortress! I am in a difficult battle right now, but I trust You. Fill me with assurance and courage as I persevere through this trial. Thank you!

May 20

The lord replied, "Look around at the nations; look and be
amazed! For I am doing something in your own day,
something you wouldn't believe even if
someone told you about it!
~Habakkuk 1:5

God sees and cares deeply about what happens on earth.
<u>Intentionally look</u> for how God is moving and you <u>*will see*</u> his
powerful handiwork! His creations and flat out miracles are
prevalent even today. You just have to open your eyes, ears,
and heart.

Dear Lord,

Your works astound me! There is no one like you. Please make me
more aware of Your Presence. Sharpen my eyesight so I can see more
of Your miracles and beautiful creation. Strengthen my hearing so I
can clearly hear Your gentle whispers. Give me an open heart and
mind so I am able to experience Your presence. Thank you Father!

May 21

This vision is for a future time. It describes the end, and it will be fulfilled. If it seems slow in coming, wait patiently, for it will surely take place. It won't be delayed.
~Habakkuk 2:3

The key words here are *it will be fulfilled, wait patiently,* and *it will surely take place.*

Waiting can be tough and nerve wrecking for anyone. The longer we're required to wait, the harder it is for us to sit still. It becomes increasingly more difficult to trust Jesus when we're waiting for something/someone that, in our minds, we need right away. We then begin to question, doubt, worry, and fear. This is no way to live, and God doesn't want you to live like this.

Twice in this verse, God reminds Habakkuk that the violence and injustice will be addressed by Him. All God's promises prove true.

The Lord declares "for surely it will take place." It will certainly happen, in His time, <u>which is perfect</u>, so why would you question that? Don't worry about what you see right in front of you. Don't doubt the Lord. Wait. Be patient. Be still. Trust in Him.

Dear God,

Please give me more patience as I wait for Your response. I know that Your timing is always best. I place all my trust in You, for You are God most High!

May 22

The sovereign lord is my strength! He makes me as surefooted
as a deer, able to tread upon the heights.
~Habakkuk 3:19

Do you ever feel as though you're walking on a tight rope,
wobbling and continuously trying to keep your balance? Do
you feel uneasy and unsteady in certain areas of your life?
Praise God, who is your strength. Those who trust in the Lord
can live triumphantly through any circumstance.

God is the One who keeps your feet firmly planted and your
spirit strong so you can *tread upon the heights.* There may come
times you stumble or fall, but take heart because God is
offering His hand to help you back up. Will you accept this
invitation and grab hold of it?

Dear God,

Thank you for keeping my feet steady and secure as I walk along this
bumpy road. I trust in You and will not fear anything that comes
my way because You are my strength, my shield, and my loving
Father.

May 23

Seek the Lord, all who are humble, and follow his commands.
Seek to do what is right and to live humbly.
~Zephaniah 2:3

If your thoughts, words, actions, and intentions are selfish and unrefined, ask Jesus Christ to humble you. God isn't looking for perfection or people who rank number one in their field. He's looking for people who strive to live righteously and have a humble heart and attitude. God extends rich grace to those who are humble.

Dear Lord,

I want nothing more than to do Your will and to remain humble. Please remove any ounce of pride, selfishness, and greed. Keep me from boasting about anything except Your love and goodness.

May 24

Those who are left will be the lowly and humble,
for it is they who trust in the name of the lord.
~Zephaniah 3:12

This verse is about God's deliverance of His people. On the day the Lord returns to render judgement, He will remove the proud and evil, but rescue all who are *lowly and humble* for they have kept their trust in Him and sought to live righteously.

We all sin and can be prideful at times. The question is, do you recognize this as sin and seek forgiveness from God? Do you repent and ask for humility?

Dear God,

Teach me what it means to be low and humble. Change me from the inside out. I want to reflect Jesus, the perfect picture of humility and love. Thank you Father!

May 25

For the lord your God is living among you.
He's a mighty savior. He'll take delight in you with gladness.
With his love, he'll calm all your fears.
He will rejoice over you with joyful songs.
~Zephaniah 3:17

This verse describes so much about God's supreme and compassionate character. He is just as alive today as he was thousands of years ago before the Bible was even written! He is our Alpha, Omega, Almighty Lord who saved our souls. He delights in us with great gladness and minimizes our fears. He is so overjoyed with us that He sings songs!

The reason why many of us don't experience His Presence is because we focus on the wrong people, materials, and/or ideas. We don't "see" or "hear" Him because we gaze into the visible world and listen to what culture says, rather than seeking Truth. When we truly understand that He is living and breathing right now, and that He is right with us every second of every day, we can relax easier.

Search for your heavenly Father earnestly and intensely and *you will* experience His presence, see His works, hear His whispers, and be at peace.

Dear Father,

Whenever I am afraid, I will turn to Your Word and pray to You because I know with certainty that Your compassion, peace, and comfort will eradicate that fear. Thank you for Your unending grace, soothing peace, and everlasting love.

May 26

Be strong, and now get to work, for I am with you,
says the lord of heaven's armies.
~Haggai 2:4

God sent Haggai to motivate the Israelites to rebuild God's temple and encourage spiritual renewal. The Lord sent this message through Haggai. He reminds them He is with them, instructing them to *be strong and get to work.*

We must stop sitting around when life throws us a curveball. Whether you personally encounter a new problem or are hit with a sudden tragedy, remember God is with you, and He is your strength. Be courageous. You have God on your side, so why do you doubt? You can do anything when you firmly trust in His power.

Whether a natural disaster strikes, an economic crisis begins, or a global issue starts to negatively impact millions of people, remember that God is in control. There is no reason to panic.

Dear Father,

When life throws me a curveball, I will turn to You. Please keep me rooted in Your truth and lend me Your strength. You are all-powerful and all-knowing, always in complete control. I trust You.

May 27

The Lord says, "Shout and rejoice, O beautiful Jerusalem,
for I am coming to live among you!"
~Zechariah 2:10

Zechariah was certain that God would live among His people
again, shining His glory throughout Jerusalem. No one knows
the day of God's return, but we do know that His Spirit dwells
among all who believe in Him!

Don't keep quiet about this. "Shout and rejoice!" Tell your
friends, family, co-workers, and even acquaintances or
strangers that the Holy Spirit lives within you (and them). Be
overjoyed and celebrate this promise.

Dear Lord,

Thank you for your Holy Spirit who comforts me. Help me become
more aware of Your presence. Tune out every noise that deafens my
spiritual ears. Unblock everything in view that clouds my spiritual
vision. I love you Lord.

May 28

Do not despise these small beginnings,
for the lord rejoices to see the work begin.
~Zechariah 4:10

Every tremendous milestone started as a tiny choice. Every CEO or power player of a company was previously a minor person in their field. Every finished painting began with a single, simple stroke of a paintbrush. Every major-league sport player had their first very practice.

All masterpieces start small. All successful and accomplished people go through their share of mistakes, problems, and sacrifices <u>before they prosper</u>.

Dear Lord,

Thank you for this small beginning! I often want to reach the end result quickly, but I know that the building of my character comes during the process. Help me to maintain a grateful attitude for every small step of progress.

May 29

This is what the Lord of Heaven's Armies says: "Judge fairly and show mercy and kindness to one another."
~Zechariah 7:9

As Christians, we're ambassadors for Christ. We represent Him here on earth. We are called to teach others the Truth and Good News, to share our testimonies, and to explain to everyone how much God loves them! We must remember to be forgiving and kind to everyone, as Jesus is, because we are His hands and feet. Above all, love others as Christ loves you.

Dear God,

Thank you for Your mercy and loving kindness that You freely give me with no strings attached. Teach me to be this way towards others! Please give me a heavenly perspective and wisdom so I remain fair, gracious, forgiving, and loving to everyone.

May 30

For I'm planting seeds of peace and prosperity among you.
The grapevines will be heavy with fruit. The earth will
produce its crops, and the heavens will release the dew.
~Zechariah 8:12

If you want God's peace, and if you want to prosper, then completely submit your entire being to your heavenly Father!

He wants an intimate relationship with you, one in which you are in continual communication with Him. He only asks that you trust His ways and timing, obey His instructions, and remain faithful to Him during **all** circumstances. Then, peace and prosperity will overflow in your life!

Dear Father,

First of all, thank you for planting seeds of peace and prosperity within my soul. You are so gracious to me. Now, Father, help me sow these seeds well so they can flourish and accomplish Your will.

May 31

Come back to the place of safety, all you prisoners who still have hope! I promise this very day that I'll repay two blessings for each of your troubles.
~Zechariah 9:12

When sheep wander from their shepherd, they become lost, confused, lonely, and vulnerable to attack. They left their place of safety, and are now exposed to evil without protection. They end up in fear and without hope. They undergo many difficulties and suffer from hardships.

We are the sheep and Jesus is our shepherd. He guides us along the path of everlasting life. He never sleeps. He watches over us constantly. The great news is that if you do wander away from him and are left lost, stuck, confused, afraid, and/or lonely, all you need to do is grasp His hand that is right there. When you accept His help, you are guided back to safety. Furthermore, He promises to give you double blessings for each trouble you faced. Jesus is *Hope* and your *refuge*. Will you turn back to Him?

Dear Jesus,

I am lost and confused. I'm in such darkness that I can't even see where to go. I feel completely stuck in this situation and don't know what to do. I'm lonely and afraid. Jesus, I want to immediately return to Your path for You are my Light and Hope. Thank you for accepting me back with compassionate, open arms every time. Thank you for the comfort, peace, and joy You freely give.

June 1

Ask the Lord for rain in the spring,
for He makes the storm clouds.
~Zechariah 10:1

This verse is an excellent reminder to ask God for whatever you need or desire because He is our ultimate provider.

Did you lose your job and are now in desperate need of an income to pay bills and support your family? Were you diagnosed with an illness and need comfort and total healing? Are you bound in anxiety and need a calmed mind and God's peace? Are you plagued by feelings of regret, shame, or unworthiness and need to be freed from these toxic thoughts? Do you need a miracle?

Whatever you need and whatever your heart desires, ask the Lord for it. He hears you and will answer you in His timing and according to His will.

Dear Lord,

I bring you all of my burdens right now and ask that You lift them off my shoulders. Take away the poisonous thoughts of shame and unworthiness and free me from shackles of anxiety and fear. Father, I know that You are more than capable of providing the miracle I need right now. I trust that You know exactly what I need and when.

June 2

By my power I'll make my people strong, and by my authority they'll go wherever they wish. I, the Lord, have spoken!
~Zechariah 10:12

Our "power" and "strength" are not created by ourselves alone. God's power is what makes us mighty and stable. This verse goes on to say that we can go wherever we wish *if* it's under God's authority. If the destination of our choosing is not aligned with His will, then He will correct our course. Stay on God's path if you want strength!

Dear Father,

I want nothing more than to do Your will. I surrender my heart and mind to You. Father, I respect Your authority and how You work in my life. Thank you for being in charge and being with me wherever I go.

June 3

*I will bring that group through the fire and make them pure. I
will refine them like silver and purify them like gold.
They will call on my name, and I will answer them.
I will say, "These are my people,"
and they will say, "The Lord is our God."
~Zechariah 13:9*

Tragedies are painful to endure. Evil is terrifying to face.
Extreme hardships can crush our strength. God promises to
not only *take you through* it, but to *refine and purify you like silver
and gold*! How amazing! With faith, call on Him and He will
not let the danger harm or destroy you.

Dear God,

*There is none like You – my rescuer from all trouble, all disease, all
fear, and all evil! Thank you for not only helping me through, but for
also polishing me into something new and beautiful.*

June 4

A son honors his father, and a servant respects his master.
If I'm your father and master,
where are the honor and respect I deserve?
~Malachi 1:6

It's important to honor and respect not only our parents and grandparents, but our boss, government leaders, and other authority figures. We ought to express respect and kindness to everyone, but because of who God is, He deserves nothing short of deep reverence and full devotion.

Don't let your selfish desires, busy lives, or excuses decrease the amount of honor and respect you show to our heavenly Father.

Dear God,

You are my Master. Although I don't understand how or why things happen, I submit to You and respect Your ways. I know You are the supreme manager of everyone and everything. Although I feel life is unfair from time to time, I know that You judge and rule righteously. God, help me to honor You more by showing respect and honor to the authority figures in my life.

June 5

I am the Lord and I do not change. That is why you
descendants of Jacob are not already destroyed.
~Malachi 3:6

Malachi was reminding the people of God's faithfulness. It is impossible for Him to break a promise and to not grant a blessing, covenant, or miracle that He said He would fulfill.

The Bible is full of His promises: to love you unconditionally, to fully forgive you and cleanse you of sin when you repent, to be with you always, and to give you eternal life in heaven. He promises us that He is *good* and always *in control*. He promises that He is our shield, therefore, we should not fear.

Relax. You have security in Him because of His faithfulness.

God is light. He is truth. He is victorious. He is love. You should be so incredibly grateful that He does not and cannot change.

Dear God,

Thank you for never changing! I can depend on You without question. Help me to rest in Your security and to focus on Your promises rather than my circumstance. I am tired of the stress and anxiety that comes from focusing on myself, personal life, changing situations, and the ups and downs of life. Help me to let go of that and grasp onto Your flawless promises and unchanging character.

June 6

*Bring all the tithes to my storehouse so there will be enough
food in my temple. If you do, I will open the windows of
heaven for you. I will pour out a blessing so great you won't
have enough room to take it in! Try it! Put me to the test!
~Malachi 3:10*

Really? Test the supreme God? Yes, He tells us to test Him on
tithing. Intentionally and generously give the first ten percent
of what you earn back to Him, and just wait to see Him *open
the windows of heaven for you.*

In regards to your finances, there will be times of prosperity as
well as times of uncertainty. It is important to remain faithful
to God even when it seems like you won't be able to make
ends meet. This is a test of faith. Will you give to Him or
choose not to? If you do, He promises to give you back so
much that you won't have room to store your blessings! The
reward is beyond anything you could ever think of. God
explicitly instructs us to tithe. Try it. What do you have to
lose?

Dear Father,

*Refill my faith when it begins to escape. I cannot see how this is
going to work out, and yet I will wait in expectation for a great
blessing because You have promised a reward beyond what I can
imagine when I remain faithful to You.*

June 7

*But for you who fear my name, the Sun of Righteousness will
rise with healing in his wings. And you will go free,
leaping with joy like calves let out to pasture.*
~Malachi 4:2

Repentance is the only proper response to sin because God's
judgment is inescapable. The Lord said those who fear
(submit to and greatly respect) Him will "rise with healing!"
They will "leap with joy" because they will experience
freedom, tranquility, and pure bliss!

Dear Lord,

*Thank you for Your unending forgiveness and grace! Thank you for
absolving my sins. You are the One who sets me free from all fear,
anxiety, guilt, shame, and negative feelings of unworthiness. I will
forever praise Your name!*

June 8

*Prove by the way you live
that you have repented of your sins and turned to God.
~Matthew 3:8*

John the Baptist prepared the people to receive Jesus. He emphasized the need to return to God through repentance – asking for forgiveness and leaving the pride, lies, and sin behind and *turning* to humble obedience to God. Mere words will not suffice.

Think of how often others don't follow through with their words. Think of how often *you* don't follow through with your words. Sometimes we say we will do something, but don't follow through, even though we initially had the best intentions to do so.

Your actions are what make your words ring true. This is especially important when it comes to turning to the Lord. One can't simply say, "I am sorry God. I turn to You." Yes, apologize and ask for forgiveness. Then *act by turning to Him.* This means spending time in the Word rather than watching television or surfing the internet. This means praying wholeheartedly on your knees to the Lord rather than sinking into poor habits with people who are negative influences. Truly *turn* to God and you will be blessed.

Dear Father,

I am so sorry for my sins. Bring to light whatever I need to do. Please help me to follow through with what I say to my family, friends, coworkers, and everyone. Grant me the strength and courage to turn to You during times of temptation. Thank you for forgiving me and embracing me each time I return to You!

June 9

You are the light of the world – like a city on a hilltop
that can't be hidden.
~Matthew 5:14

Jesus is the Light of the world, and praise God that absolutely nothing can extinguish His radiant Light. You can either be in a situation where you still have some visibility but the Light is dimmed, or, you can be surrounded by pitch black, terrified and hopeless. In either scenario, call out "Jesus."

Jesus is like a spot light, accentuating the path He wants you to take. He will illuminate your path and help you out of the frightening darkness.

Dear Jesus,

You are my Light who shines constantly, never even flickering. Thank you for showing me a clear, bright path to follow. Thank you for rescuing me from the darkness that surrounds me. I can fully trust your brilliant flare that both brings me Light and brightens my path.

June 10

Let your good deeds shine out for all to see, so that everyone
will praise your heavenly father.
~Matthew 5:16

The key words here are *so that*. We are called to "do good
deeds" **so that God is glorified,** not so that we are praised or
noticed.

Honor the Lord by serving others without having your own
agenda. Give generously without being greedy or proud. Love
and encourage others rather than seeking attention for
yourself. Help those in need before yourself. Do these things
not for recognition, but so that others will praise God.

Dear Father,

I desire to serve selflessly, give generously, and live humbly. I invite
you into my heart this very moment to alter it and make it stronger.
Father, please bless me with a heart like Your Son has. I am called to
be the hands and feet of Jesus, so grant me a humble, loving, serving
heart. In Jesus name, amen.

June 11

When you pray, go away by yourself, shut the door behind you, and pray to your Father in private. Then your father, who sees everything, will reward you.
~Matthew 6:6

Too many of our prayers are brief or rushed. To make any relationship personal or intimate, you need to devote time to that relationship. Spend one on one time with the person to get to know him/her on a deeper level. Don't rush your time with others, especially time with God. Time with your Heavenly Father is so precious.

Your personal relationship with Jesus Christ must come before all other relationships in your life! It's up to you to flourish that relationship because God is the same yesterday, today, and forever. He is always there, pouring out endless love and grace, waiting for you.

When you sit quietly with God, privately, He revitalizes your soul. He isn't looking for perfection. He's looking for persistence in wholeheartedly seeking Him.

Dear Heavenly Father,

I want nothing more than to know You better, hear Your voice, see Your works, and live according to Your will! Our time together is precious. Keep distractions and temptations away so I can focus on growing our relationship. Thank you for being fully devoted to me.

June 12

Can all your worries add a single moment to your life?
~Matthew 6:27

Worry and anxiety don't benefit us one bit! They are in fact
very skilled at one thing in particular. They are excellent faith
blockers. They do a fantastic job at keeping you in an endless
cycle that you continue to repeat and/or in a sticky web that
you cannot escape. In these cycles and webs, faith becomes
exhausted and is impaired. The good news is that there is
freedom readily available – Jesus.

Despite how vicious the cycle seems and how frightening
your situation is, <u>make the choice to place your trust in Jesus</u>
because there is *no fear in His love.* Worry and anxiety cannot
survive in His presence. Fearful thoughts melt away. Do not
worry. Trust Jesus. Period.

Dear Jesus,

I am done with worrying. It has never proven effective or beneficial.
I will seek You. Give me the courage to surrender my anxiety
entirely so I can place total trust in You. Thank You, Jesus, for being
my serenity.

June 13

*Seek the kingdom of God above all else and live righteously,
and He will give you everything you need.*
~Matthew 6:33

Chasing success, fame, money, a dream, or a spouse in order
to fill a void will not yield the results you're looking for. If you
feel like you *need* those things or other material possessions,
you are incorrect. You only need God. All things flow from
Him. Freedom is found in Him. He loves unconditionally.

Jesus is the only One who can fill the void in your soul, and
His Father provides *exactly what you need*. You can stop
"needing" things and relax.

Since God is infinite and abundantly accessible, desiring Him
above everything is simply the best way to live. He is your
ultimate provider.

Dear Lord,

*I will keep my eyes fixed on You in both the good times and the bad.
When my life is flowing smoothly and I'm in a season of prosperity,
I will seek Your kingdom and thank You for providing such
wonderful blessings. When my life seems to spin out of control, I
will seek Your kingdom and thank You for giving me another
opportunity to trust You more. Lord, You are all that I need.*

June 14

Keep on asking, and you'll receive what you ask for.
Keep on seeking, and you'll find.
Keep on knocking, and the door will be opened to you.
~Matthew 7:7

Never give up praying. God hears and answers. The response may not be what you wanted or hoped for, but praise the Lord for that because *He knows exactly what you need.* We can't see the whole picture. Our minds are so narrow and insignificant compared to His. The answer may not come when you want or when you feel it should come, but praise the Lord yet again! *His timing is always perfect.*

Never give up seeking God. Spend time in the Word, worship, and talk to Him even when you don't *feel* anything.

Wait attentively and in expectation for Him to work in your life.

Dear Father,

I present my request to You once again, and will continue praying until You respond. I accept, respect, and trust Your answers and Your timing because You are my Almighty Father. Thank You for listening to me and answering me right when I need.

June 15

If you cling to your life, you'll lose it,
but if you give up your life for me, you'll find it.
~Matthew 10:39

Jesus' love is so deep that He chose to suffer a crucifixion for us. He gave up his life so that we may have eternal life.

Cling to Jesus, who is Hope and Life, and follow Him. Then, you will find your life! Regularly strive to please Him, letting go of your life and living the life He has for you. Heaven is your permanent home. Knowing this makes surrendering your life for Him much easier.

Dear Jesus,

Thank you for giving up your life so that I may live eternally in heaven. I surrender my life to you. I give you my heart, mind, and soul. I hand over every goal, dream, and desire that I have and choose to follow You. Jesus, help me with surrendering all to You.

June 16

Take my yoke upon you. Let me teach you, because I'm humble and gentle at heart, and you'll find rest for your souls.
~Matthew 11:29

Let the Lord teach you. Don't question Him or analyze His instructions too deeply. Don't ignore any of His directions.

This world is our classroom. God is our Teacher and the Bible is our textbook. His word, promises, and endless love provide comfort for our confused, anxious minds, giving us the rest we so desperately need. <u>Allow</u> Him to teach you.

Dear God,

Thank you for teaching me how You want me to love others. Thank you for teaching me what forgiveness, grace, and mercy look like. Thank you for building my character through hardships and tragedies. Please give me an open mind and teachable spirit so I can continue learning and growing.

June 17

To those who listen to my teaching, more understanding will
be given, and they'll have an abundance of knowledge.
But for those who aren't listening, even what little
understanding they have will be taken away from them.
~Matthew 13:12

Gazing too long at your problem results in confusion, restlessness, anxiety, and/or fear. This creates an open pathway for the enemy to come in and flood your mind with more lies, doubts, worries, and fears because your attention is more focused on those thoughts than God.

Our enemy is continuously on the prowl, ready to distract us from God, which is why it is absolutely crucial to remain grounded in Truth. Listen to the Lord's instructions, and He will bless you with understanding and knowledge!

Don't wear yourself out by analyzing your problem. Don't exert all your energy into doing what culture and the world say. Stop. Listen to the Lord Almighty, for it is He who gives you wisdom and understanding.

Dear God,

Thank you for Your instructions. I desire to grow in understanding. Please make my ears sensitive to the Holy Spirit so that I can really hear what You are teaching me.

June 18

Jesus said, "You don't have enough faith. I tell you the truth,
if you had faith even as small as a mustard seed, you could
say to this mountain, 'Move from here to there,'
and it would move. Nothing would be impossible."
~Matthew 17:20

This verse speaks volumes. Ponder on the **power of faith!**
Jesus said a mountain can move when faith is demonstrated.

Voice trust in your majestic Father frequently. When your
faith shakes, you veer off the path He intends for you to be on.
Look to God, regardless of your circumstance or feelings, and
whisper "I trust you Jesus."

Taking steps of faith and depending on God opens the door to
abundant blessings!

Dear Jesus,

I confess that I have lost some faith. I ask that you fill me up Lord!
Replace my doubts with total trust and confidence in You. Eliminate
the anxieties, fears, insecurities, and anything that else that causes
my faith to falter.

June 19

Jesus looked intently and said, "Humanly speaking, it's impossible. But with God everything is possible!"
~Matthew 19:26

Your path may *appear* to be barricaded with no way forward. You may feel it's impossible to overcome your current circumstance. It may seem like there is no way to heal from the sharp pains and deep-seated grief within.

Fortunately, this is just what it *feels like* and how things *appear.* It looks and feels utterly impossible to get through or survive.

Take heart, because with God *everything is possible.*

Dear Lord,

This seems impossible, so I choose to look to You, who can make anything possible. Help me to look beyond the visible and past my current feelings. I place my trust in You!

June 20

To those who use well what they're given, even more will be given, and they will have an abundance. But from those who do nothing, even what little they have will be taken away.
~Matthew 25:29

First of all, be thankful for whatever you have. Focusing on what you don't have, or on anything negative for that matter, darkens your mind.

Second of all, use what you've been given wisely. Would you trust someone who wastes money you loaned them or who was careless with your belongings? Use *all* that you have been given, including your gifts and talents, money, time, and material possessions, productively. After all, nothing "belongs" to you anyway. Everything on earth and in heaven belongs to our tremendous God. You are just managing what's His. Take great care of it all and use it for good (serving, helping the poor & needy, giving generously, using your gifts to enhance His kingdom) <u>so that more will be given to you.</u>

Dear God,

Thank you for everything You have given me! I am forever grateful. Help me to manage my gifts, finances, and time productively for Your kingdom.

June 21

*Teach these new disciples to obey all the commands
I gave you. And be sure of this:
I am with you always, even to the end of age.*
~Matthew 28:20

God tells us to **be sure** that He is always with us! The thoughts that God is not listening or with you are from the enemy.

Throw out all doubts and insecurities right when you think of them. <u>Replace them with God's promises.</u> He is omnipresent and is waiting patiently for us to do our part – call to Him and express our dependence on Him.

Dear Lord,

Thank you for being with me constantly, through all of the highs and lows, all the happiness and suffering, and all the blessings and battles. You are my everlasting Father whom I can rely on in all situations. Thank you!

June 22

I baptize you with water,
but he will baptize you with the Holy Spirit.
~Mark 1:8

John the Baptist announced that people should be baptized to show that they indeed have repented and turned to God for forgiveness. The baptism of Jesus brought the gift of the Holy Spirit, through whom sinful people become God's children.

Dear Jesus,

You are my Savior! Thank you for giving me Your Holy Spirit, who teaches me right from wrong and guides me along Your path. Whenever I face difficult choices, please grant me discernment so that I know I am making a wise choice that honors You.

June 23

Jesus said, "Pay close attention to what you hear. The closer
you listen, the more understanding you'll be given
and you'll receive even more."
~Mark 4:24

How can you hear well if your ears are clogged with gossip,
lies, and discouragement? How can you hear well if Satan's
attacks of shame, guilt, and fear flood your ears?

Don't pay attention to those terrible voices. Tune your ears to
Jesus! He knows your pain, fear, and anxious thoughts, and is
primed to pour His peace into your mind and soul!

As you spend time with Jesus, the Lord's promises will sink
into your mind. You will be able to hear the Holy Spirit louder
and clearer. You will be strengthened and prepared for
whatever is about to come.

Dear Jesus,

Thank you for routinely communicating with me. Unplug my ears. I
want to hear Your voice so I can gain understanding. Do not allow
anything to block my view of You or Your miracles. I will lean in
with all my heart to Your word and through prayer so that I may
hear what You are teaching me.

June 24

Jesus told them, "Don't be afraid. Just have faith."
~Mark 5:36

If you truly trust God, nothing can separate you from his peace, and everything that you endure is put to good use. **Trust wholeheartedly because He is in control.** He fixes shattered hearts, heals the deepest wounds, repairs and restores relationships, transforms minds, and rejuvenates hopeless souls.

When times are problematic or demanding, have even more faith. God blesses those who look beyond their situations and towards Him above!

Dear God,

I am done being afraid. Please free me from the bondage of fear. Thank you for instilling courage and confident trust within my soul.

June 25

Jesus said, "What do you mean 'If I can?'
Anything is possible if a person believes!"
~Mark 9:23

Trust and believe in the Lord with <u>every fiber of your being</u>. Don't just believe He *can* cure your fatal disease, solve your irreparable problem, or restore your broken relationship. Believe He <u>will!</u> Doubt is out. Plug in your faith.

Dear Jesus,

You have proven time and time again that doubt is unnecessary. You remind me repeatedly that with You, anything is possible. I praise Your powerful, glorious, wonderful name! Thank you for making the impossible possible.

June 26

Didn't you ever read this in the scriptures? "The stone that the builders rejected has now become the cornerstone."
~Mark 12:10

Although many people followed and loved Jesus those thousands of years ago, many rejected him. Did he let them mess with his mind? Did he let that rejection overtake him? Absolutely not.

Jesus, although rejected by many, is our essential cornerstone. He holds our lives in His hands. He gives us life, guides us throughout our time on earth, and protects us from the enemy.

You will be rejected at some point in your life. Keep your eyes fixed on Jesus. He has a unique way of turning rejection and failures into success.

Dear Jesus,

Thank you for being my cornerstone whom I can rely on forever. I trust You will use any evil intentions against me for Your Father's good will.

June 27

The second is equally important:
Love your neighbor as yourself.
~Mark 12:31

Yes, of course it is quite difficult to show kindness and love to someone who hurt you. It can be painful to show forgiveness and love to someone who wounded you or a loved one. It can be strenuous to show patience and love to someone who repeats the same sin.

Regardless of all that and despite how we feel, Jesus tells us the second commandment is **equally important** as loving God with all your heart, and that is to love your neighbor as yourself.

Act like Jesus. How in the world can we do that when it "feels" so wrong to love that "undeserving person?" We can do this through prayer and allowing God to work within us, transforming our mind and helping us love and forgive.

Dear God,

I desire to obey all of Your commands. Teach me how to love my neighbor in ways that honor You. Holy Spirit, speak through me as I talk to people. Father, control my mind and soak my heart.

June 28

And since you don't know when that time will come,
be on guard! Stay alert!
~Mark 13:33

No one knows the day or hour when Jesus Christ is returning. There won't be any warnings or signs. This is why we must be vigilant. Do not wander away from the Lord into the shadows and darkness. Do not surround yourself with people or activities who will corrupt your mind, steering you away from the Truth.

Stay absorbed in the Word and in communication with God, your Father in heaven.

Dear Lord,

Keep my mind from ever doubting Your Word and give me the courage to defend it. Keep my feet firmly planted on the path of Life. When I am shaken, keep me attentive to You so I am not impaired in any way.

June 29

And he told them, "Go into all the world
and preach the Good News to everyone."
~Mark 16:15

The "good news" is referring to the fact that God brings
salvation! God sent Jesus Christ to die for our sins, and *anyone*
who believes in God, declares with their mouth He is their
savior, and turns from their old ways to follow Jesus' is saved.
Amen!

How will anyone know this good news unless we tell them
about it? How will anyone experience God's pure love or
become aware of His awe-inspiring presence if we don't teach
them about His faithfulness and miracles from the Bible and
our lives? How will they know that the Holy Spirit is their
guide and gateway to Him?

There are too many lost souls in this fallen world for you to sit
on the sidelines enjoying your own relationship with God. Get
up and help save as many people as you can!

Dear God,

Give me the boldness to joyfully teach others about You. Holy Spirit,
speak through me in ways the people I'm talking to can easily
understand. I will be your vessel here on earth, bringing as many
people to salvation as I can.

June 30

And the disciples went everywhere and preached,
and the lord worked through them,
confirming what they said by many miraculous signs.
~Mark 16:20

There's no reason at all to feel nervous when sharing your testimony or talking about your personal relationship with the Lord. You do not need to worry about having the right words when trying to teach others about God.

Cling to His promises and boldly teach the Truth in love. You will be surprised at the great confidence that the Holy Spirit will deliver to you.

Dear Holy Spirit,

Help me share the gospel with confidence. Give me a gentle, soft, loving tone while speaking, and let the exact words that need to be heard in that moment be spoken through me.

July 1

The word of God will never fail.
~Luke 1:37

Intentionally or not, people let us down. Relationships can be neglected or abandoned. What we hear from others or read can prove to be gossip and lies.

God will never forsake you. It's not even a possibility, so do not fear. The Bible and His promises remain true. His Word never fails. It's the one and only thing that will never fluctuate, deteriorate, or let us down. And yet, we often rely on and trust our friends or loved ones so much that we become shattered when they fail us or when we fail them.

Rely on and trust your Heavenly Father. Spend your precious time with the never-failing word of God.

Dear Father,

Thank you for being by my side at all times. Thank you for teaching me Truth through the Holy Bible. Help me to center my entire life around Your promises and instructions.

July 2

For the mighty one is holy,
and he has done great things for me.
~Luke 1:49

The joy and glory are God's, but He gives them to you as you live in His presence in thankfulness and trust. Rejoice during both trials and triumphs, for God is working *in and through you!* **Remember** all the blessings He gladly gave you and praise His holy name!

He is your provider, giving you exactly what you need right when you need it. He is your mighty defender, guarding you from evil. He is your strength, revitalizing your soul and infusing energy so you can press on. He is your peace, instilling calmness during times of anxiety, stress, and fear. He is your miraculous physician, healing everything from a minor cold to a terminal illness. All that you have which you consider blessings (family, friends, career, home, car, etc.) are from the Lord above! Therefore, reminisce on all the great things He has done for you and all blessings He has given you.

Dear Lord,

Your name is glorious and Your works are remarkable! Thank you for everything You have done for me, are doing for me, and will do for me.

July 3

Jesus answered them, "Healthy people don't need a doctor. Sick people do. I have come to call not those who think they're righteous, but those who know they're sinners."
~Luke 5:31

You cannot live a fulfilled life without Jesus Christ. How many times have you tried doing something on your own and failed? Do you keep getting "stuck" in life? Are you wandering in the wilderness, lost and confused? Do you continue moving down an endless spiral?

Jesus is the solution! Stop trying to survive on your own or seek your own selfish desires. You may experience temporary contentment, but you will never be completely fulfilled if Jesus isn't the foundation of your life!

Dear Jesus,

Teach me to be as loving, forgiving, and gracious as you. Grant me a passion for leading the sick and hurting to you so they can be saved and develop a personal relationship with you, Jesus!

July 4

Love your enemies! Do good to them.
Lend to them without expecting to be repaid.
Then your reward from heaven will be very great, and you'll
truly be acting as children of the Most High,
for He is kind to those who are unthankful and wicked.
~Luke 6:35

Our gracious King is kind and forgiving to those who are ungrateful and evil, so we must also treat our enemies with kindness and forgive them for their actions. Why? Because the Lord instructs us to and because we are called to be the hands & feet of Jesus Christ.

If we can put aside our human perspective, and instead focus on developing a heavenly view, then we receive some relief, and "our reward in heaven will be very great."

Dear God,

I cannot love my enemies without Your help. Please give me a gracious and forgiving heart. Father, help me to show them kindness and mercy even when they mistreat me.

July 5

*For all that's secret will eventually be brought into the open,
and everything that's concealed will be brought to light
and made known to all.*
~Luke 8:17

The Truth always captures secrets and lies! Living a lie or
hiding things allows stress and fear to run straight to your
mind. Instead of living in secret, confess your sins and repent,
for it will be known eventually.

God already knows everything about You. He loves you
regardless of your performance. As soon as you declare "I
confess of my sins. Jesus, please forgive me," He showers you
with mercy.

Dear Jesus,

*I am done living in secret and keeping things from you. I confess all
of my sinful words, actions, and thoughts – everything I consciously
am aware of, but also any sin that I am unaware of. Jesus, I am
sorry. I turn to you! Help me recognize how and when I sin, and
give me the boldness to confess right then and there. Thank you for
always forgiving me!*

July 6

Jesus replied, "Even more blessed are all who hear
the word of God and put it into practice."
~Luke 11:28

Results come after an *action* takes place. To lose weight, you must change your diet and exercise. To graduate from college, you must study hard. To prove to someone that you're reliable and loyal, you must *do what you say.*

To receive God's amazing and generous blessings, you must *put the Word into practice* by both obeying His commands and applying His principles and instructions to your life <u>daily.</u> Be intentional in this endeavor every day.

Dear Jesus,

As I read God's Holy Word, tune out every noise except the Holy Spirit's voice. Do not allow distractions to keep me from hearing You and obeying Your instructions.

July 7

Jesus explained, "Beware! Guard against every kind of greed.
Life isn't measured by how much you own."
~Luke 12:15

If you honestly have a heavenly perspective and know where
your permanent home is, then lavish homes, fancy cars,
beautiful clothes and jewelry, successful businesses, and all
the money in the world will mean absolutely nothing to you.
When you can understand and submit to the fact that the real
assessment of your life directly relates to your personal
relationship with Jesus Christ, then you will not be so hungry
for those "awesome" things that you "need."

Instead of striving for more "stuff," which is only available to
you during your short time on earth, spend your energy and
focus on being a humble, faithful servant of the Lord. Teach
others about Him, show everyone love and forgiveness even
if, in your mind, they don't deserve it. Help those in need. Use
your gifts and talents to glorify God! You will certainly be
blessed. Your mind can't even fathom the rewards and
treasures you'll receive both here on earth and in heaven
when you dedicate your life to living for God!

Dear Lord,

Please replace cravings for things that are meaningless to You for
what is purposeful, worthwhile, and important to You! Do not allow
greed to grow in my heart. Eliminate anything that attacks
selflessness and humility. Thank you!

July 8

Here's the lesson: Use your worldly resources to benefit others and make friends. Then, when your possessions are gone, they will welcome you to an eternal home.
~Luke 16:9

Not many of us seek to benefit others *before* ourselves. We often think or ask, "What's in it for me?" and "Why should I do that for you?"

The real questions we should be thinking of and asking are:
- "How can I use my gifts and talents to enhance you/this problem?"
- "How can I use what I know to teach you?"
- "How can I use my prior experience and resources to help you improve?"
- "What else can I do to benefit you?"

Committing your life to following Jesus involves doing your best to live like Him. Well, <u>Jesus always thought of others before himself</u> and used His power to benefit them, not himself.

Dear Jesus,

Thank you for teaching me this important lesson! Show me how I can use my gifts and talents to grow others and glorify You. Show me how I can use my knowledge to teach others. Show me how I can use my experience and resources to help others improve. Give me a desire to strive to benefit others before myself.

July 9

So the Word became human and made his home among us.
He was full of unfailing love and faithfulness.
And we have seen his glory, the glory of
the Father's one and only Son.
~John 1:14

Your best protection against stress and anxiety are knowing God's word and what He says about You. If you want your relationship with God to flourish, make it a priority to study and meditate on His truth, and do your very best to live righteously.

You can know with certainty that you can trust God's Word because of His perfect faithfulness.

Dear God,

Your Word is alive and powerful. I ask that You please make it clear to me as I read it. Please present Your promises and instructions in ways that I can easily understand. Thank you for teaching me Truth.

July 10

No one needed to tell him about human nature,
for he knew what was in each person's heart.
~John 2 25

No human can dive into the depths of another's heart, seeing their true desires and motives. Only our majestic, all knowing God knows our innermost being. In fact, He knows us better than we know ourselves, so who are we to question His path for us? He knows exactly what will nurture our heart, so who are we to seek our own pleasures without consulting Him first?

Dear God,

You know my heart's desires. If I want something that does not align with your will, please change the desire of my heart. God, saturate my heart with Your desires, Your plans, and Your will for my life!

July 11

So, don't be surprised when I say, 'You must be born again.'
~John 3:7

Humans give birth to human life. The Holy Spirit gives birth to spiritual life. To enter God's kingdom, you must be born again of water and the spirit: baptized and saved. Baptism is simply an outward expression of what you believe internally. It is a symbol to others showing that you believe Jesus is your Savior. *Anyone* who believes in God, believes that He sent His Son Jesus to die on the cross to rescue us from death, and confesses with their mouth that Jesus is their Savior <u>is given eternal life.</u> Halleluiah and amen!

Dear Jesus,

Thank you for redeeming my life through your death on the cross. Now that the Holy Spirit resides in me, Jesus, help me to remain sensitive to it and help me respond to its directions and instructions.

July 12

He must become greater and greater,
and I must become less and less.
~John 3:30

When success and prosperity arrive, recognize and give praise to the Lord before yourself. Resist the temptation to brag about yourself. Give glory and thanksgiving to God!

Terminate selfish thoughts. Stop striving to be the center of attention. Rather, maintain a humble attitude in everything you do. Verbally express thankfulness to your Father and exalt Him. Shout praises to Him for all to hear.

Dear Lord,

I magnify your name because there is none like You. If a prideful thought or action begins, stop it in its tracks immediately. Replace it with humility. You deserve all glory, honor, and praise!

July 13

Jesus said, "But those who drink the water I give will never be thirsty again. It becomes a fresh, bubbling spring within them, giving them eternal life."
~John 4:14

We often feel unfulfilled, discontent, or incomplete in one or more areas of our lives. We have a void that never seems to be satisfied. If you don't have a solid relationship with God, you end up trying to fill this emptiness through relationships with people (healthy or unhealthy), opportunities (safe or unsafe), and/or sinful activities that deep down you know is harmful.

The answer to any void is Jesus Christ! If you genuinely surrender yourself to Him and make the choice to follow Him, you will receive blessings beyond belief and inexpressible joy! You will never feel *thirsty* for anything when you have an intimate relationship with Jesus because He installs a *fresh, bubbling spring within* so you never feel dry or empty. How incredible! Praise the Lord!

Dear Jesus,

I choose to follow You and obey Your instructions. With my whole heart, I will do my best to reflect your Light and Love to everyone in my life. I will strive to live out Your instructions and teach them to others so they can experience Your presence as well. Thank you for continually nourishing my soul!

July 14

Jesus told them, "This is the only work God wants from you; believe in the one He sent."
~John 6:29

There is a misconception that we enter heaven by being a good person, doing good deeds and following all the rules. Of course, God instructs us to live righteously and obey, but that is not the ticket to heaven. We enter heaven when we believe that Jesus is Christ and our Savior.

God can accomplish significantly more both in and through you when you decide to ignore culture and rebuke the enemy's lies, and instead choose to *believe Jesus* and who God says you are. Release your independence and rely on Him.

Dear Lord,

I believe in You and will follow wherever you lead, even if the path scares or confuses me. You know what's best and are in control. I trust Your plans for my life.

July 15

Jesus told him, "I entered this world to render judgment – to give sight to the blind and show those who think they see that they are blind."
~John 9:39

Physical blindness isn't the only type of blindness. Many people are spiritually blind. Jesus came to glorify his father's name and perform outstanding miracles so people can see spiritually. Furthermore, he came to teach those who *think* they see righteously that they're actually blind to what God is trying to show them - His unfailing love, forgiveness, incredible peace, and the Holy Spirit.

Dear Lord,

Please do not allow my spiritual sight to be blocked or taken away. Holy Spirit, point out the Truth to me today and every day. Help me teach the truth in love to others. Speak through me, saying just what it is they need to hear from You. I am your vessel.

July 16

*They won't follow a stranger; they will run from him
because they don't know his voice.
~John 10:5*

Jesus is explaining here that he is the good shepherd. All of
the *true sheep* who go through the gate to follow him will not
only be saved and be able to roam freely in good pastures, but
they will *know his voice*. They will not follow a stranger
because they do not believe in that voice. They follow Jesus,
the voice of truth.

Similarly, if you give up your life and wholeheartedly follow
Jesus along His path and into the *good pastures* He has for you,
then you will be able to distinguish His voice from others and
you will not be manipulated by false shepherds.

Dear Jesus,

*Thank you for leading me into good pastures! Please bless me with
wisdom and discernment so that I can know with certainty whether I
am hearing from You or not.*

July 17

The thief's purpose is to steal and kill and destroy. My purpose is to give them a rich and satisfying life!
~John 10:10

It is crucial to know Satan's tactics and plans as well as God's so you can distinguish the two.

Satan, the father of lies, loves to steal from you. He manipulates your mind, stealing clarity, understanding, and peace. He is the master of deception. He can easily make a lie or sin seem fine. He presents temptation in just the perfect way and at just the right time to catch you off guard. His goal is to destroy your relationship with God. His plans are to destroy your joy and peace!

God's goal is to give you a <u>rich and satisfying life.</u> He wants you to live in peace and to experience unspeakable joy!

Whereas Satan is here to take away life, God gives us an abundant life.

Dear God,

Please keep my spiritual eyes and ears on high alert at all times so I can quickly recognize Satan's attacks. Give me the courage to face him with confidence and to fight the good fight with You and Your word. Thank you Father!

July 18

*"Your love for one another will prove to the world
that you're my disciples."*
~John 13:35

This is in Jesus' final farewell. Before He left, He wanted to ensure He reminded them of the most important commandment: love others as He loves them. Jesus explained that their love towards others will prove they are His disciples.

Show sympathy for those who are ill and hurting. Give compassion to the hopeless and to those whose hearts are crushed. Demonstrate kindness towards the helpless, poor, and needy. Love everyone as Jesus loves you. Doing such is the evidence that you are a child of God.

Dear God,

Thank you for loving me even at my worst and for showing such great compassion when I am broken and hurting. Father, help me extend Your love and grace that's within me towards others! Help me be more compassionate, caring, and loving to my family, friends, coworkers, strangers, and enemies.

July 19

When everything's ready, I will come and get you,
so that you will always be with me where I am.
~John 14:3

The key words here are *when everything's ready*. Blessings and breakthroughs will come *when everything is ready*. Relief and rescue will come *when everything is ready*. God calls us home to heaven when everything's ready.

Relax and live in the present moment where God meets you. Don't dwell on the past or worry about the future. Refuse to let negative thoughts of unworthiness, shame, or guilt knock you down. All of the "What if" thoughts about the future will only bring you anxiety. Remain in the present moment with God!

Do your best day in and day out to be the hands and feet of Jesus. Focus on viewing the world through a heavenly lens. Remain in the Word and communicate with God throughout each day. Relax. Trust in God's timing because everything will happen according to His good, pleasing will *when everything is ready.*

Dear Lord,

Thank you for being in complete control! Please help me live in the present moment with you so I don't concentrate on and abide in the past. Keep me in the present so I don't become fixated on anxious thoughts. I believe that You take care of everyone and everything at the perfect time and I trust You.

July 20

*Jesus added, "You can ask for anything in my name, and I'll
do it, so that the Son can bring glory to the Father."
~John 14:13*

How is your life going right now? Is it going pretty well, or is
there a hardship or tragedy you're struggling to get through?
Whether you need comfort, support, guidance, wisdom,
discernment, renewed energy, strength, hope, or peace, *ask
God for anything and He will do it.* This is truly amazing!

Present your requests to the Lord and He answers. If it is
aligned with His will, your request will be granted. Relax even
if your request isn't granted because the Lord knows what is
best for you. Never doubt His answers or His timing.

When a prayer is answered, whether large or small, it's critical
to remember who answered it and what great power He has.
To glorify God, share your answered prayer with others.

Dear God,

*I lay all my requests at Your feet right now. I know that You reply
with exactly what I need and that You respond in Your time. I trust
You Father!*

July 21

I'm leaving you with a gift – peace of mind and heart. And the peace I give is a gift the world can't give.
So don't be troubled or afraid.
~John 14:27

Jesus taught us that his Father sent the Holy Spirit as His advocate. This divine, righteous, faultless Spirit is what teaches and guides us. Jesus also assured us that He's leaving us with *peace of mind and heart*. This incredible gift has no comparison! Having peace from God himself is better than anything you can think of. He reminds us once again: "do not be troubled or afraid."

Dear Lord,

I can't thank you enough for Your peace that You freely give me every day. When doubt tries to gain a foothold in my mind, I will gaze to You and seek Your peace! When anxiety tries to make roots within my soul, I will focus on Your peace!

July 22

Jesus taught them, "If you remain in me and my words remain in you, you may ask for anything you want, and it'll be granted!"
~John 15:7

Draw near to Him with a grateful heart. Occupy your mind with thanking Him. Strive to become more and more aware of His presence. If you remain in God, <u>then</u> you'll receive whatever you ask for as long as it's in God's will, because nothing can ever change His will and purpose for your life.

Meditate on God's instructions and promises. Let them soak into your heart and be at the forefront of your mind.

Dear God,

Thank you for sending Your Holy Spirit to abide in my heart, mind, and soul. Please make a permanent home in my heart and mind for Your Word to rest. Keep distractions and temptations from having any influence on Your Truth.

July 23

Jesus stated, "You didn't choose me. I chose you. I appointed you to go and produce lasting fruit, so that the Father will give you whatever you ask for, using my name."
~John 15:16

Isn't it astounding that Jesus chose us? Despite our sins, flaws, and mistakes, He chose us. Knowing that some of us would disobey, rebel, and decide not to follow Him and go our own way, He chose us. Even though some of us waltz with the enemy, giving into temptations and the flesh, He chose us.

Jesus appointed His followers to produce lasting fruit by teaching the gospel and reflecting His love. Those who call Jesus their Savior and walk on His path have been *set apart* to lead as many people as possible to salvation to enhance God's kingdom.

Dear Jesus,

Thank you for choosing me despite all of my flaws and mistakes. Thank you for granting me eternal life even though I sin. Help me enhance Your Father's kingdom as I follow along Your path.

July 24

Jesus told them, "Here on earth you'll have many trials and sorrows. But take heart because I've overcome the world."
~John 16:33

Don't be surprised by the enemy's fiery attacks on your mind. He's trying to destroy your relationship with God. This is spiritual warfare. Do not be afraid because God has already *overcome the world.*

God won't allow circumstances to overwhelm you if you remain focused on His presence, lean into and trust His promises, and continuously pray. We receive the right amount of hardship, so there is no need to retract. Trust in your unshakeable protector.

If you're in the middle of a major challenge, thank God anyway because He will either equip you with the tools necessary to solve it or take care of the problem Himself. Praise God even during times of oppression, misery, or grief because He is giving you another opportunity to trust Him more.

Dear God,

Thank you for the difficulties of life. I know that You are strengthening my faith, growing my trust in You, and enhancing our personal relationship. When disaster strikes, suffering comes, or anxiety and fear flood in, I will run to You, my unmistakable and miraculous Lord.

July 25

They don't belong to this world any more than I do.
~John 17:16

Wow, this is powerful! In Jesus' final prayer to his Father, he said we don't belong to this world any more than he did. Our permanent home is in heaven with God.

Jesus is so devoted to us that he communicates with God on our behalf! He asked God to keep us safe from the evil one. He also earnestly prayed that God will make us holy by the Truth and teach us the Word so that we can understand "the truth will set us free." Jesus is clearly our best friend, so loyal, trustworthy, and loving.

Dear Jesus,

Thank you for being my best friend and praying to our Father when I don't know what to say. Please teach me the Truth in a straightforward, precise way so I can easily understand and apply it.

July 26

No wonder my heart is glad and my tongue shouts his praises!
My body rests in hope.
~Acts 2:26

Rejoice in all God's done for you, and His light will shine
through you into the world.

When plagued with a problem, look above and seek a
heavenly perspective. You will then see the dilemma begin to
fade. **With Jesus**, it is possible to have joy during difficulties.

Dear Lord,

It is well with my soul. You make my heart glad and give me rest.
Thank you! Continue to pour hope and peace into me, especially in
times of uncertainty, chaos, or tragedy.

July 27

We believe that we are all saved the same way,
by the undeserved grace of the lord Jesus.
~Acts 15:11

You can't earn your way into heaven and nothing you've done can disqualify you from entering heaven, no matter how dark or deep that sin is! God has given you the *free gift* of eternal life *through grace* alone.

Your past sins and mistakes don't matter. Your current situation and faults don't matter. Your future offenses and missteps don't matter. You've already passed from death to life when you accepted Jesus as your personal savior.

Dear God,

Thank you for giving me eternal life for free. There is no gift that exceeds this! I will forever praise Your wonderful name, for you are a good, good Father.

July 28

Human hands can't serve his needs for he has no needs. He himself gives life and breath to everything, and he satisfies every need.
~Acts 17:25

You *need* everything and God needs nothing. Realize that you're completely dependent on Him. You wouldn't even be able to breathe without your mighty Father! You must always rely on the One who satisfies every need.

Relax. You can stop chasing people, money, success, or things to try to satisfy your desires. Do not waste any more time or exert any more energy in pursuing meaningless things.

Fortunately, there is only one person we need to pursue, and that is God. He *fulfills every need, satisfies every desire, and refills every void.* **He is the way, the Truth, and life.** You don't have to search high and low for someone or something, trying to feel better. You don't need to drive around through multiple avenues trying to feel better. There is only one person and one place you need to look: God in heaven. When you genuinely know this and believe it without question, you will be in total serenity.

Dear Lord,

You provide every need and satisfy every desire I have. You fill my emptiness with Your loving kindness, peace, joy, and hope. Make this truth so apparent to me that I never feel inclined to search for anyone or anything other than You.

July 29

Jesus explained, "So guard yourselves and God's people.
Feed and shepherd God's flock – his church purchased
with his own blood – over which the Holy Spirit
has appointed you as leaders."
~Acts 20:28

The Holy Spirit assigned us to lead the church and care for God's flock. Be on guard, for the enemy is always trying to take your gaze off Jesus and onto him instead.

We must unite and be ready to protect ourselves and each other in trials and battles.

Dear God,

Keep my church and community of believers strong in faith, courageous, wise in Truth, and prepared with our spiritual armor so we can stand firm against Satan's attacks. Make us aware of His schemes so we can conquer them. Point out how he's trying to manipulate our minds and give us the scripture necessary to be victorious over his lies and tactics.

July 30

*This good news tells us how God makes us right in his sight.
This is accomplished from start to finish by faith.*
~Romans 1:17

We won't be made righteous by our works. God makes us
righteous when we place complete and genuine faith in Him.
This applies to all humanity. We are all sinners and fall short
of God's standards. But, our gracious God willingly and
gladly makes us right in His sight when we have faith in Him.

Faith is complete trust and confidence in someone or
something. It is believing in the unseen. We often doubt and
worry because of our current situation or how things appear.
This can surely delay a blessing. God will wait as long as it
takes for faith to give life. *Have faith.* Believe not only that He
can answer your prayers, but that He will.

Dear Father,

*Please nurture my faith so it can flourish! Keep it steady so that I do
not stumble when life catches me off guard with a dilemma or
tragedy. Keep it strong so that worry, fear, and doubt remain locked
out of my mind!*

July 31

Don't you see how wonderfully kind, tolerant and patient God is with you? Does this mean nothing to you? Can't you see that his kindness is intended to turn you from your sin?
~Romans 2:4

The Bible abounds with lessons to learn. Repeatedly, God shows kindness to all, including those who are wicked. He forgives all sin when people repent and demonstrates patience towards everybody. God models this behavior for us to follow. Yes, it is difficult to be kind, tolerant, and patient to those who, in our eyes, don't deserve it. He instructs us to anyway because that is how He treats you.

Selfishness cripples the spirit. Love rebuilds the spirit. Be kind and patient to everyone, and at all times. The Lord will bless you.

Dear Father,

Thank you for modeling righteous behavior. Help me be more sympathetic towards others when they're hurting. Help me to be courteous even when they are not. Give me an extra amount of grace and compassion so I can hand them over to others.

August 1

We can rejoice, too, when we run into problems and trials,
for we know that they help us develop endurance.
~Romans 5:3

Instead of complaining about a problem, thank God for it.
Rather than feeling anxious or afraid, seek Him and you will
be soothed by His peaceful Presence. Don't let chaos and
tribulations tie you up in stressful knots. *Relax and look* for
what God is trying to show and/or teach you.

Even if there is a monstrous mountain ahead with no clear or
sensible way to approach it, thank Him. If you are diagnosed
with an "incurable" disease, smack in the middle of an
"impossible situation," or stuck in utter darkness, thank Him.

Adversity is a part of life. Rather than trying to control or fix a
problem, focus on seeking the Lord's Presence and
perspective. Praising Him in the middle of such hardships
develops endurance, chisels away negative parts of your
character, and builds your trust in God.

Dear God,

Thank you for the problems in my life. I know that You use
everything for Your good purposes. When I face the most difficult
times, help me let go of the desire to control or fix the problem and to
instead surrender to You!

August 2

*For since our friendship with God was restored by the death
of his Son while we were still his enemies,
we will certainly be saved through the life of his Son.
~Romans 5:10*

God demonstrated his amazing, profound love for us by
sending Jesus to die *while we were still sinning.* Through Jesus'
blood, God made us pure in His sight.

Rejoice in the personal relationship you have with your
heavenly Father because of Jesus your Savior.

Dear Lord,

*Thank you for your unconditional love! Thank you for sending Your
only Son to be crucified on the cross so that I may have a
relationship with You and live eternally in heaven.*

August 3

Sin is no longer your master,
for you no longer live under the requirements of the law.
Instead, you live under the freedom of God's grace.
~Romans 6:14

Paul explains that our relationship with sin is different because of Christ's death. To be "dead to sin" does not mean to never sin or never make mistakes. Paul teaches us that Christians do not have to live as helpless slaves to sin. They can *choose not to sin.*

When Jesus died on the cross, we died to the power that sin previously had in our former selves. Jesus' death demolished sin's power! Do not allow sin to control the way you live. Refuse to let sinful desires win.

Dear God,

I am simply awe struck by your unending grace! Thank you for freeing me from the sin that once enslaved me.

August 4

*Letting your sinful nature control your mind leads to death,
but letting the Spirit control your mind
leads to life and peace.
~Romans 8:6*

The enemy is a scheming manipulator who attacks our minds because he knows a mind not focused on God's truth will be more susceptible to his tactics. He presents temptations in sneaky ways that <u>do not appear </u>to be temptations or sin. He deceives us and twists the Truth so smoothly. No one wants to fall to the enemy's vicious advances!

The Holy Spirit is *champion of peace.* He's our guide to all that is right, beautiful, and peaceful in this world.

Dear Lord,

Please keep my conscious clear of debris so I can realize when the enemy is trying to deceive or manipulate me. I refuse to let Satan control my mind or influence me in any way. Father, I invite your Holy Spirit in to take total control of my mind forever!

August 5

And we know that God causes everything to work together for the good of those who love God and are called according to his purpose for them.
~Romans 8:28

Relax. Don't be afraid. Even when you feel like you can't catch a breath, remember that God is sustaining you and is in control. If you feel as though you can't even get up because of the endless, exhausting burdens weighing you down, remember that God will joyfully carry them all. If you or a loved one is suffering, remember that God continually extends His compassion and healing. If you're stuck in the dark and cannot find an escape route, remember that Jesus' light is always illuminating and His hand is available for you to grab hold of.

Not a single tear or moment of anguish is disregarded. God mysteriously crafts good out of even the most difficult and painful circumstances. Persevere with prayer and keep your eyes fixed upon the Lord even in the very midst of your deepest pain and toughest challenges.

Our heavenly Father is the One who turns sorrow into joy. He *transforms anxiety into peace*. He comforts, soothes, and completely relieves our anguish. Accept how He is working, lean on His word and strength, and remain in communication with Him through prayer.

Dear Lord,

Thank you for remaining in control. I trust that this is for good. Please give me the energy and strength to persevere in prayer. Do not allow my current circumstance to influence my thoughts or heart! Instill a heavenly perspective in my mind, especially right now Father. I submit to Your ways and trust in You. Let Your glory shine during this time!

August 6

How great are God's riches, wisdom, and knowledge!
How impossible it is for us to understand
his decisions and his ways!
~Romans 11:33

A spinning mind that tries to figure everything out can make you deaf to God's voice. Instead of planning compulsively and trying to analyze how God works, simply <u>submit to His ways and obey</u>. Yes, obey even when the instruction or direction makes no sense at all, when it doesn't seem fair, and when you don't understand the reason behind it.

We will never understand His thoughts or ways, nor will we ever be able to truly grasp the depth of His unending love and mercy, but we can experience His amazing peace when we surrender our entire being to His ways, accepting His will and thanking Him for everything!

Dear Heavenly Father,

I respect the ways You are working in my life. Help me to accept everything You do through and for me with a joyful heart and positive attitude. I trust in Your Sovereignty and decisions.

August 7

Don't copy the behavior and customs of this world,
but let God transform you into a new person by
changing the way you think. Then you'll learn to know God's
will for you, which is good and pleasing and perfect.
~Romans 12:2

It is tempting to listen to the voices of culture and mimic
behaviors of those around us. We often compare ourselves to
others, and judge people based on appearances, possessions,
and/or success. These harmful thoughts steer us away from
godly living and guide us right towards selfishness. Trying to
find your calling in life through imitating other people,
striving to always please others, or behaving like others just to
"fit in" with society will just lead you on an ineffective,
unfruitful path.

Let God transform you into a new person by changing the way you
think. Stop comparing, judging, and thinking negatively. Give
up your strategies and allow God to work in your heart. He
leads you on a successful, worthy, meaningful path full of
unimaginable blessings.

Dear Lord,

I surrender to You! Please grant me a new and pure mindset that
maintains a heavenly perspective. I know that Your plans for me are
best. Please align my motives with Your good, pleasing, and perfect
will.

August 8

Don't let evil conquer you, but conquer evil by doing good.
~Romans 12:21

You will face trials, fear, disasters, and times of crisis during this life, but take heart! God is always with you, and He uses what was meant to harm you for good. Refuse to be defeated by these hardships and terrors. Believe that you can actually **conquer** them, no matter how impossible it may seem, with the Lord Almighty! <u>With Him, you can do absolutely anything.</u>

How do you overcome wickedness, corruption, and hatred? By *doing good*. Pay back those who disrespect you with *kindness and love*. *Forgive* those who hurt you. *Help* your enemies when they struggle. Be a glowing light in times of darkness.

Dear God,

Please give me courage to stand up tall against all evil so I may defend myself by fighting with what is good in Your eyes - kindness, love, grace, mercy, and forgiveness. Help me appreciate times of darkness. Help me respect those who mistreat me, forgive those who cause corruption, and be gracious towards those who afflict me.

August 9

Therefore, as the Scriptures say,
"If you want to boast, boast only about the Lord."
~1 Corinthians 1:31

Paul explains here that we were not wise in the world's eyes, and we lacked power and wealth when God called us. He blessed the low and humble with prosperity. A pure heart has no room for pride. Since Jesus made us holy and freed us from sin, the only thing we can boast about is Him!

Dear Jesus,

Thank you for rescuing me from death. You are perfection. No one and nothing can ever come close to comparing with You. You represent complete wisdom, absolute love, and unequaled peace. You embody supreme faith, impeccable grace, and matchless power.

August 10

That is what the Scriptures mean when they say, "No eye has seen, no ear has heard, and no mind has imagined what God has prepared for those who love him."
~1 Corinthians 2:9

Paul tells us here that the leaders did not understand God's plan, which was previously made hidden. If they had, they would not have crucified His Son.

God revealed His plan through His Holy Spirit. We cannot possibly know anyone else's thoughts; only that person's spirit knows his/her thoughts. Only the Holy Spirit knows God's thoughts.

We received God's spirit so we can know the wonderful things God has freely given us! Praise the Lord! We don't deserve anything, yet God gladly blesses us abundantly. The Spirit is not only our guide to righteousness, but also our lens to God's grace, love, and power.

Dear Father,

Thank you for the gift of Your Holy Spirit! Please make me more aware of its Presence so I can know Your will, the wonderful plans You have for me, and where you are leading me.

August 11

Stop deceiving yourselves. If you think you are wise by this world's standards, you need to become a fool to be truly wise.
~1 Corinthians 3:18

If you feel God is making a mistake in your life, that is incorrect. If you think His path for you is wrong, you should re-read His unfailing Word again. If you think His plan and purpose for you aren't good, you need to change your perspective from your mere human view to a godly view.

Wisdom of this world, pride, and thinking you know what's right/best more than God are each so far from the truth. Our thoughts will never surmount to God's secure, steady, and flawless ways!

Dear God,

I am sorry for thinking that I know what's best and believing in my plans more than Yours. Erase my pride. Take away the desire to know everything and give me a teachable spirit. Help me to pause and <u>listen to Your voice</u> – true wisdom.

August 12

But for us, there is one God, the Father, by whom all things were created, and for whom we live. And there is one Lord, Jesus Christ, through whom all things were created, and through whom we live.
~1 Corinthians 8:6

God the Father is our *Author* because He created us. He is our *Founder* because He created the world and everything in it. He is our *Master* because He is in total control of everyone and everything at all times. <u>We are to live for Him.</u>

God created everything *through* Jesus, His Son. Jesus was born as a human to fulfill his Father's mission of redeeming us from our sins. <u>We are to shine the Light in this darkened world.</u>

Dear God,

Thank you for creating me. Thank you for sacrificing Your only Son to die for me. I submit my dreams, goals, and desires to Your will because I trust in Your divine promises.

August 13

Don't you realize that in a race everyone runs,
but only one person gets the prize? So run to win!
~1 Corinthians 9:24

What is your dream job? What does your perfect home look
like and where would it be? What is your heart's biggest
desire? Once you realize what that is, don't you rush towards
it with all your strength? Because you want it so badly, you
direct all your attention and might towards landing that job,
buying that home, and doing whatever it takes to receive your
heart's desire.

Our supreme, loving, faithful God is above all! He should
without a doubt be first in your life. *Run to Him*, for He is your
eternal prize. When you earnestly chase after His Presence
and seek His will, blessings will certainly come your way and
the desires of your heart will be given.

Dear Father,

Please give me the stamina and power to run after You every day.
Strengthen my spiritual muscles and keep my faith fully charged.
Do not allow anyone or anything to discourage me, weakening my
endurance. Fill me with a positive, heavenly perspective and keep me
motivated to purse You.

August 14

God works in different ways,
but it's the same God who does the work in all of us.
~1 Corinthians 12:6

Be on guard of comparing yourself to others. Be aware of
judging people and situations. You never know what someone
may be dealing or struggling with. Certainly, you never know
the Lord's plans or directions for others.

God has a unique path for each of us individually, so how can
we all receive the same blessings, opportunities, or gifts in
life?

Dear God,

Thank you for remaining constant. I can rely on You without an
ounce of worry or doubt because of Your faithfulness, grace, mercy,
and great love, all of which never falter. Please barricade judgment
from my mind and terminate thoughts of comparison.

August 15

For God isn't a God of disorder, but of peace,
as in all the meetings of God's holy people.
~1 Corinthians 14:33

Being organized and detailed are good qualities to have. Planning well is beneficial. Be careful that it doesn't turn into an idol. When the planning becomes excessive and begins to be your main focus, your attention can drift from God. Trying to control what will happen and attempting to fix people and/or situations will take your eyes off of the One who is in control.

God is Peace! Turn to your heavenly Father to experience the unexplainable, simply incredible sense of peace you're longing for. He is waiting for you.

Dear God,

Thank you for Your sound Peace. Please do not allow my to-do lists and mental check lists precede seeking You. Do not let the details of my plan be the focal point of my mind. Bless me with flexibility and contentment so that when my plans don't work out, I still feel Your Peace.

August 16

So, my dear brothers and sisters, be strong and immovable.
Always work enthusiastically for the Lord, for you know that
nothing you do for the Lord is ever useless.
~1 Corinthians 15:58

If God calls you somewhere, then run there without
hesitating! If He calls you to do something, obey without
question!

Dedicate your heart and mind to whatever His plan is, despite
what anyone else tells you or how you feel initially. If you've
been convicted by God, then obey Him enthusiastically
without wondering what others are thinking or worrying
what anyone says.

Working for the Lord will benefit you in more ways than you
can ever fathom.

Dear Jesus,

Please breathe strength and perseverance into my soul so that I can
press on. Plant enthusiasm within me as I work for You. Thank you
for using my works for God's ultimate will.

August 17

And do everything with love.
~1 Corinthians 16:14

In Paul's final instructions of this letter, he reminds us to be on guard and brave. He encourages us to anchor our heart to faith. Last, but not least, he emphasizes that we should *do everything with love.*

To honestly and accurately be the hands and feet of Jesus, all that we say and do must be done with *love.*

Dear God,

I want to reflect Your great love and Jesus' radiant light. Nurture the love within me so I can show others the gracious, forgiving, beautiful love that You show me. Make my tone gentle and soothing when I speak. Instill within me a desire to serve and help others before myself.

August 18

He comforts us in all our troubles <u>so that</u> we can comfort others. When they are troubled, we will be able to give them the same comfort God has given us.
~2 Corinthians 1:4

The Lord comforts us not just to relieve our pain, revitalize our hope, soothe our nerves, and calm our fears, but *so that we can comfort others.*

Jesus Christ came to heal the sick, mend the broken hearted, and help all those in need. As disciples of Christ, we are set apart to shower others with comfort and love. We are able to do this because of God's endless compassion!

Dear God,

Thank you for alleviating my discomfort, lifting my burdens, and cheering me up whenever I need. Thank you for extending compassion to me every day.

August 19

*But thank God! He has made us his captives
and continues to lead us along in Christ's triumphal
procession. Now he uses us to spread the knowledge of Christ
everywhere, like a sweet perfume.*
~2 Corinthians 2:14

Paul discusses his ministry as an apostle teaching the Good News. He thanks God that He chose him to be part of Christ's triumphal procession. Paul is grateful for the *privilege* to speak about Jesus.

It is both an honor and privilege to be able to teach others about God, Jesus Christ, and the Holy Spirit. Have a thankful attitude like Paul did.

When we do our part by teaching the Good News, a pleasing fragrance fills the air! What is this Good News? The Good News is that by God's grace, we were given eternal life when Jesus died on the cross for our sins. God is always with us and works in our lives through His Holy Spirit.

Dear Father,

Please give me confidence to boldly proclaim the Good News to others. Help me teach Your Word with love. Have me present Truth in ways that are easily understood.

August 20

Since this new way gives us such confidence,
we can be very bold.
~2 Corinthians 3:12

Here, Paul is teaching about the glory of the new covenant. The old covenant brought condemnation, but the new one brings glory because God made us righteous and gave us new life through the Holy Spirit.

Pray boldly! When obeying God's instructions, do so fearlessly. Wherever the Spirit leads you, walk in confidence, for the Spirit always leads us along God's perfect path. Leave personal feelings and desires at the door and keep your focus on God, the magnificent Master of everything on earth and in heaven.

Dear God,

I trust in Your everlasting promises and faithfulness. Please do not allow discouragement or fear to influence me. Help me to boldly give you my requests and courageously follow where You lead.

August 21

We're hunted down, but never abandoned by God.
We get knocked down, but we're not destroyed.
~2 Corinthians 4:9

We are fragile. We can fall when challenges come. We can give into temptation. Our faith can be shaken during times of uncertainty. We can trip even while walking along Jesus' path. Enemies can stalk us and evil can be in our shadows. But, praise the Lord because we will not be destroyed. His glorious power is what keeps us from crumbling.

Dear Lord,

Thank you for picking me up when I fall and steadying my faith when it quivers. Thank you for protecting me from harm and giving me the victory over my enemies. I will forever praise Your name!

August 22

For our present troubles are small and won't last very long.
Yet they produce for us a glory that vastly outweighs
them and will last forever!
~2 Corinthians 4:17

Rest assured that God will never let a situation overwhelm you if you gaze to Him. For every setback you have, whether it be physical, emotional, or spiritual, know that there is a transformation taking place within you.

When a crisis arrives, we either accept the situation and cling to faith or we descend into worry, fear, and/or hopelessness. Instead of concentrating on the situation, fixate your mind on what you can't see. Your Savior will stabilize your faith, fill you with hope, and give you peace.

Hang in there! Keep looking to Jesus. The final outcome will outweigh all the tears you cried and problems you faced. When you endure tragedy and trouble with faith and trust in God, the blessings and rewards you will receive later, either on earth and in heaven, are marvelous!

Dear Lord,

I need You. Please give me strength to press on during challenges. Please give me confidence to move through the darkness. Implant a thankful attitude within me so I can praise You even during the toughest times.

August 23

We use God's mighty weapons, not worldly weapons, to
knock down the strongholds of human reasoning
and to destroy false arguments.
~2 Corinthians 10:4

Using worldly reasoning and weapons can shatter you. Rely on scripture and prayer when you're in a battle. God's word will keep you secure and balanced. Prayer keeps you connected with your sovereign Lord.

Paul goes on to say that we ought to *capture thoughts and teach them to obey Christ.* When a toxic thought enters your mind, acknowledge it, capture it, and rebuke it in Jesus name. Replace it with Truth found in scripture.

Dear God,

Please help me foster harmony with others. I want to confidently teach Your Word and fearlessly pray for others. Help me uphold Your word at all times. Lord, make me more aware of the toxic thoughts and lies that enter my mind, and give me confidence to capture them and let them go!

August 24

Jesus gave his life for our sins, just as God our father planned,
in order to rescue us from this evil world in which we live.
~Galatians 1:4

How sweet are the words *just as God our father planned*! God's
plan is foolproof and unblemished. We cannot fully
comprehend the width and depth of His love and mercy.
Praise the Lord that everything happens in His time.

God's plan will always prevail. We have free will and are able
to make our own plans, but God's purposes for your life will
come to pass. Amazing peace comes when you surrender your
plans to Him.

Dear Heavenly Father,

I release my plans to you. Reveal Your plan for my life. Tell me
where You want me to go. Show me what You want me to do. Teach
me what You want me to learn. Make me into the person You want
me to be. I trust You!

August 25

But we who live by the Spirit eagerly wait to receive by faith the righteousness God has promised to us.
~Galatians 5:5

God's spirit will never lead people to sin. The problem is that because of our sinful and hardheaded nature, we can lack the wisdom of knowing the right thing to do.

His Holy Spirit teaches us what is right and guides us to do what pleases God. Furthermore, when we allow the Spirit to steer the wheel of our minds, words, and actions, we can wait confidently and more patiently for the blessings promised by our Father!

Dear Lord,

I choose to rely on Your Spirit that resides in me. Thank you for cleansing me of all sin, making me blameless in Your sight. You are my rock, my salvation, and my life!

August 26

Dear brothers and sisters, if another believer is overcome
by some sin, you who are godly should gently
and humbly help that person back onto the right path.
And, be careful not to fall into the same temptation yourself.
~Galatians 6:1

Note the words *gently and humbly*. Criticizing, demeaning, and yelling at others do not reflect Jesus. Arrogantly pointing out others' wrongs or roughly forcing them to change does not reflect God's love.

We are all sinners. We need to be gracious, compassionate, and forgiving towards one another, especially when we fall short. To help others return to the right path, refer to God's living Word because it is secure! Read scripture and heed to the Holy Spirit.

Dear God,

When I recognize that one of my family members or friends is overwhelmed with sin, help me extend extra compassion upon him/her. When someone is stuck in a sin cycle, help me tenderly guide him/her back to You by lovingly reminding them of Your promises. Intercept Satan's schemes before they reach me.

August 27

So, let's not get tired of doing what's good. At just the right time, we'll reap a harvest of blessing if we don't give up.
~Galatians 6:9

It's definitely a challenge to forgive the wicked, help the selfish, or love the ill-tempered, but it is crucial to be persistent in doing good because you represent Christ. Always do good, remembering you're serving the Lord.

Be consistent in showing the fruits of the spirit: love, joy, peace, patience, kindness, goodness, faithfulness, gentleness, and self-control. *At just the right time,* abundant blessings will come your way!

Be patient during your season of waiting. God blesses those who trust Him during the wait. Be patient during times of tragedy. God will restore your joy and peace as you cling to faith during the pain. It may seem as though the season will never end. You may start to beg God to relieve you immediately, but accept your situation and trust Him because His timing is always perfect.

Dear Father,

Please do not let me ever grow weary of doing what's right and good in Your eyes. I seek to please You above all else! Please keep my faith alive and stable during the dark times. Give me peace and confidence in You during my dry seasons.

August 28

Even before he made the world, God loved us and chose us in Christ to be holy and without fault in his eyes.
~Ephesians 1:4

Meditate what God says about you. In His eyes, you are worthy, righteous, beautiful, forgiven, and loved.

Our Father's perfect love is not subject to variation. What varies is our awareness of His presence. When your self-esteem depreciates, remember you're a child of a Father who's overflowing love, compassion, and forgiveness are dedicated to you!

Dear Lord,

Thank you for choosing me in spite of my failures and sin. Instruct me how to love others unconditionally, just as they are. Help me to see others as You see them.

August 29

He is so rich in kindness and grace that he purchased our
freedom with the blood of his Son and forgave our sins.
~Ephesians 1:7

Would you purchase a product that was damaged or corrupt?
Of course not. Would you invest your time and energy in an
unworthy relationship? No way.

God bought us, knowing full well that we are broken and
sinful! Clearly, our graceful, loving Father deserves **all** of our
heart, mind, and soul.

Dear God,

I cherish my relationship with You. Train me to give others the
amazing grace You freely give me. Polish my heart and mind. Coach
me to be more like You.

August 30

*The Spirit is God's guarantee that He will give us the
inheritance He promised and that
He has purchased us to be his own people.
He did this so we would praise and glorify him.
~Ephesians 1:14*

The Holy Spirit, which navigates our life, <u>guarantees</u> us that
we will have eternal life. This amazing gift is not for our own
sake. It was given freely *so that we can glorify God.* It is
guaranteed – bonded, sealed, and certain. Halleluiah!

It cost God everything to purchase us and call us His own. His
one and only son, Jesus Christ, had to die on the cross so that
we could live in heaven for all eternity.

Dear Lord,

*Thank you for the free gift of salvation! Thank you for fulfilling
every promise. I pray that all I do glorifies You and shows others
Your beautiful light.*

August 31

Together, we are his house, built on the foundation
of the apostles and the prophets.
And the cornerstone is Christ Jesus himself.
~Ephesians 2:20

Church is not a building. Christians, as citizens of heaven, are the church.

A cornerstone is the most important piece of a building's foundation, and Jesus is our unshakable cornerstone. The apostles and prophets laid the foundation (message of Christ & the Good News), and the cornerstone that keeps us strong and sound is Jesus! There is no reason to fear.

Dear Lord,

I ask that You keep Your children united together in faith. Establish deep roots that are firmly planted in Your Word into each of us so we can fight the good fight well. When chaos strikes, tragedy crashes in, or Satan's lies attack, we will grip tightly to Jesus Christ, our cornerstone.

September 1

*Now all glory to God, who is able, through his mighty power
at work within us, to accomplish
infinitely more than we might ask or think!*
~Ephesians 3:20

It is by Christ's magnificent power and abilities that we are
able to persevere through hardships and tragedies, conquer
the impossible, and regain joy, peace, and strength. *Everything
is possible with the Lord.*

He can instantly make a way when there seems to be no clear
path to take. He can immediately turn an impossible situation
180 degrees around, making it possible right before your eyes.
He can easily take an obstacle in front of you that leaves you
in despair because you see no solution or way of overcoming
it and turn it into something small that you breeze right over.
He can and He will.

Not only does He make the impossible possible, but He
accomplishes His miracles, signs, and wonders *through us*. We
can't even begin to comprehend what we're capable of when
God works through us!

Dear Lord,

*Thank you for demonstrating your glorious power and wonderful
works by making the impossible possible. Use me as Your vessel to
accomplish Your great works! I surrender to You.*

September 2

Always be humble and gentle. Be patient with each other, making allowance for each other's faults because of your love.
~Ephesians 4:2

We are each unpolished, having various flaws. We all make mistakes. Strive to treat everyone as Jesus does – with humility, gentleness, patience, and love.

This does not always come easily. Jesus is the model we are to learn from. He loves, forgives, and is patient <u>with everyone</u> despite the number of mistakes made or sins committed.

Dear Jesus,

Thank you for teaching me what true humility, patience, and forgiveness look like. Please help me offer the kind of patience and forgiveness You constantly bestow to me. Help me look past others' flaws and mistakes.

September 3

*As each part does its own special work, it helps the other
parts grow, so that the whole body is healthy
and growing and full of love.*
~Ephesians 4:16

Our organs in our physical bodies work together to perform vital functions. Each player on a team has his/her own strengths, and to increase chances of victory, they must work well together.

As a child of God, you play a significant role in helping Christ's body flourish. We must strive to live in harmony with each other by speaking His Truth in love and growing more like Christ daily.

Dear Lord,

Show me how I can use my unique gifts and talents to grow Your kingdom. Teach me how to work effectively with others so that we all flourish in Your love. To You be the glory!

September 4

Don't act thoughtlessly, but understand
what the Lord wants you to do.
~Ephesians 5:17

Rushing into a relationship or job opportunity, making impulse purchases on major expenses, or suddenly dropping everything to move somewhere new without asking God first is not wise.

Yes, it's important to seek advice from knowledgeable, experienced, godly men and women. Of course, you may ask your loved ones for guidance. But, it is crucial to remember to seek the Lord's will for your life. Talk to Him first and wait patiently for Him to answer.

It's far better to wait for understanding from the Lord than to jump into something based on your own or others' desires, thoughts, or understanding.

Dear God,

Please help me refrain from rushing into something without talking to You first. Bless me with true wisdom and discernment so I am able to make decisions that align with Your will.

September 5

*Work with enthusiasm, as though you were working
for the Lord rather than for people.*
~Ephesians 6:7

Try your best to remember the fact that you are on earth only
temporarily. Heaven is your eternal home. The Lord God
Almighty is your master, for He is in charge and in control of
everyone and everything. *Everything* you do is for Him, so
maintain a hard work ethic and put forth your best effort.

Life can be draining. Physical exhaustion and emotional pain
causes great affliction. Anxiety and stress can come at any
moment. Take heart and persevere, working with enthusiasm
for the Lord, because it is He who will revitalize your soul.
God rewards those who are faithful to Him.

Dear Heavenly Father,

*Please refresh my enthusiasm so I can continue to work hard and
endure difficult times. Thank you for always providing exactly what
I need right when I need it.*

September 6

Therefore, put on every piece of God's armor
so you will be able to resist the enemy in the time of evil.
~Ephesians 6:13

We should not consider other people our enemies. Obstruction, hostility, and opposition are from the spiritual world. Evil and wickedness are present all over the world today because of the sin of man, but we do not need to fear because Christ has authority over our enemies and has already conquered Satan.

It is essential to be prepared and protected against the evil that surrounds you. Fortunately, God has given us reliable armor: the belt of truth, breastplate of righteousness, shoes of peace, shield of faith, helmet of salvation, and sword of the spirit. Stand upright with scripture. Walk righteously with God. Focus on being ruled by His peace. Keep your faith strong to deter harmful attacks. Protect your mind by remembering Jesus saved you. And, fight evil with God's promises and truths.

Putting on God's armor should be your top priority every morning.

Dear God,

Thank you for giving me dependable armor which prepares me to face corruption. Please give me courage so I can face my enemies straight on. Help me to never forget any pieces of Your armor.

September 7

And I'm certain that God, who began the good work within you, will continue his work until it's finally finished on the day when Christ Jesus returns.
~Philippians 1:6

When a situation doesn't turn out as you had hoped or you just cannot seem to escape the darkness, it becomes easier for doubt to take over you mind. You may question when or if your efforts will yield results. You may start to doubt if the dream God gave you that you began chasing after will ever be reached. You may wonder why interruptions and setbacks keep your goals from being accomplished.

When God transforms you from within through building your character, softening your heart, and/or giving you a heavenly perspective, the process can be slow and/or painful. This is *for good* and He *will finish the work He began.*

Relax. Lean on God's promises, not your own understanding. His plan will come to pass! If He began a work within or through you, He will continue managing it until it is finished. You can be certain of this.

Dear God,

Please keep me composed and calm as I wait for You to complete the good work You began in me. I know that You bring good out of my pain and heartache, and I trust that Your timing is best.

September 8

Above all, you must live as citizens of heaven,
conducting yourselves in a manner worthy of the Good News
about Christ. Then, whether I come and see you again
or only hear about you, I'll know that you are
standing together with one spirit and one purpose,
fighting together for the faith, which is the Good News.
~Philippians 1:27

Think of the world you currently live in as foreign. As a follower of Jesus, heaven is your final destination, which is why Paul urges here to *live as a citizen of heaven.* Charming, beautiful words are void without action. Behave in ways that please the Lord: serving others joyfully, giving generously, remaining faithful to Him, sharing the gospel with others, and helping those in need without thinking "What's in it for me?"

We are in a constant battle against the unseen, spiritual forces of evil, and we are to fight the "good fight of faith" together. This means overcoming evil by keeping your eyes fixed on Jesus, relying on scripture, and not losing hope or faith in the midst of the battle!

Dear Jesus,

Point out all areas where I am not acting as a citizen of heaven, and teach me whatever I need to learn. Help me teach others what living righteously looks like in a loving way. Keep my faith full at all times, but especially in the midst of adversity.

September 9

Open your eyes to those around you so you can see who needs care. Unclog your ears so you can hear those calling out for help. Stop looking only inward for what you want or need, and focus on those right in front of you who *need Jesus.* You are His ambassador called to show others His love.

Dear Lord,

Block pride, greed, and selfishness from making a home within my soul. Give me spiritual eyes and ears, and a selfless heart so I can truly be the hands and feet of Jesus by loving others as He loves me.

September 10

*Hold firmly to the word of life; then, on the day of Christ's
return, I will be proud that I didn't run the race in vain
and that my work was not useless.*
~Philippians 2:16

Paul frequently refers to God's faithfulness while reminding
Christians to remain faithful as well. The Bible is full of life-
giving words, encouraging promises, hope, Jesus' miraculous
wonders, and God's unfailing love. Don't ever take it for
granted. You must understand how powerful the living word
is. Cling to it with all your heart, mind, and soul so that you're
prepared for tough times.

Dear God,

*Thank you for your unending faithfulness and limitless compassion.
I choose to cling to Truth. Please ignite a burning desire within me
to hold firmly to the word of life.*

September 11

I press on to reach the end of the race and receive the heavenly prize for which God, through Christ Jesus, is calling us.
~Philippians 3:14

Have you ever created a fantastic plan and laid it all out or set this great goal, and then a curve ball strikes out of nowhere! <u>The key is to press on.</u> When life catches you by surprise, continue to pursue Jesus and stay on His path.

Road blocks can be on any path, and they do present a challenge. You are left frustrated or worried. You wonder if it's better to go right through them, go around them somehow, or turn back around. Listen to what God is telling you, and if He is telling you to move forward, then keep going no matter what it looks like or how you feel because He is Your strength and peace. If He gives you a way to go around and overcome the road block, then do so. If He tells you to change directions, obey.

Never give up. Live your life on earth as if you're in a race to God's kingdom which is where you'll receive the incomparable prize of eternity with Jesus.

Dear Lord,

Infuse my bones with energy so I can proceed along Your path and stand firm in trials. Fill my mind with a heavenly perspective so I remain focused on You.

September 12

Always be full of joy in the Lord. I say it again - rejoice!
~Philippians 4:4

Joy flows effortlessly when things are relaxed and fluent. The challenge comes when our routine is interrupted, our plans are thwarted, or tragedy strikes.

Remind yourself that His ways and thoughts are higher than yours. Instead of allowing the enemy or a situation to deplete your joy, keep your eyes fixed on Jesus (our source of joy).

God is either teaching you something, purifying your heart, improving your character, strengthening your faith, drawing you closer to Him, and/or reminding you of your dependency on Him.

Accept the situation. Trust Him. Praise Him through the storm.

Dear Father,

Do not allow the enemy to steal my joy. I may not understand why I'm going through this, but I accept it and trust You. If it's in Your will for me to know why, please reveal Your purpose for this situation. If not, please give me the peace of just knowing You are in control.

September 13

Don't worry about anything; instead, pray about everything.
Tell God what you need, and thank him for all he has done.
~Philippians 4:6

The human mind naturally worries when finances are tight, natural disasters strike, illness or suffering comes, or when we are running on empty unsure of how we will get through.

Worry doesn't benefit you at all. There is no point in "walking on eggshells," working yourself up in the snares of anxiety. This is no way to live, nor does Jesus want you to live in such a fearful state. He gave us a spirit of confidence.

Dear Jesus,

Help me to surrender everything to You. <u>Fill me with confident trust</u> in You so that worry does not make a home within my mind. Build a guardrail within me to prevent anxiety and fear from coming in.

September 14

*Keep putting into practice all you learned and received from
me -everything you heard from me and saw me doing.
Then the God of peace will be with you.
~Philippians 4:9*

Jesus tells us to practice what we learn and apply what we
receive (grace, love, compassion, patience, wisdom). Only
when we practice what we learn from Him will we physically
feel His tranquil peace.

Dear Lord,

*Thank you for being the exemplary role model for us all to learn
from. Thank you for giving me the Holy Spirit who helps me hear
from You. Thank you for Your word, fellowship with believers, and
the endless mercy, grace, forgiveness, and love You constantly give
so freely. Teach me how to apply Your instructions and how to truly
live out a Christian life.*

September 15

Christ is the visible image of the invisible God. He existed before anything was created and is supreme over all creation.
~Colossians 1:15

Just because something is unobservable and imperceptible, that doesn't make it nonexistent. Even though God may be invisible with the naked eye, He is there indeed - yesterday, today, and forever.

Born as a human, Jesus Christ represents his Father, our God in heaven. As a man, he was visible to those living in his time, and they were able to believe in God in heaven because of the miracles, signs, and wonders Jesus performed.

Dear God,

I ask that the Holy Spirit shift my focus from wanting to "see it to believe it" to pure faith, where I believe wholeheartedly without seeing it. I believe in You. I trust You. I love You.

September 16

For through him God created everything in the heavenly
realms and on earth. He made the things we can see
and the things we can't see, such as thrones, kingdoms, rulers,
and authorities in the unseen world. Everything was created
through him and for him.
~Colossians 1:16

Our Master created man from the dirt off the ground, which He also created. Every blade of grass, ray of sunshine, insect and animal, beautiful landforms and oceans, the galaxy, and everything on and in the entire world was created by Him! How extraordinary!

Furthermore, everything was created *for Him and for His glory!*

Dear God,

Your beautiful and unbelievable creations astound me! Help me to recognize Your power and glory in the ordinary as well the extraordinary. I praise Your name above all names.

September 17

Yet now he has reconciled you to himself through the death of
Christ in his physical body. As a result, he has brought you
into his own presence, and you are holy and blameless
as you stand before him without a single fault.
~Colossians 1:22

Despite how sinful and worthless you feel, remind yourself of
this lovely truth: Jesus Christ lived as a human so that his
physical body could die for us. When He took His last breath,
we were made holy and blameless, cleansed to be as pure as
snow.

Your past does not define you, so refuse to remain in the trap
of shame and guilt. Focusing on past mistakes, failures, and
sin is just what the enemy wants because he knows that will
drift your attention away from God and/or allow you to fall
into doubting your true identity in Christ.

God sees you as pure and worthy. You are already forgiven
and unconditionally loved. Repent to the Lord, confessing
your sins, and He will forgive you no matter what.

Dear Heavenly Father,

Thank you for sending Jesus to cleanse me of sin. Thank you for
granting new mercies for me every morning. If I begin to focus on
my past mistakes, failures, sins, or Satan's lies, please bring me back
to the present moment with You and immediately remind me of who
You say I am – worthy, loved, and forgiven.

September 18

In Him lie hidden all the treasures of wisdom and knowledge.
~Colossians 2:3

True *wisdom* cannot be found in people or things. You can read and memorize textbooks and scripture. You can become an expert in your field. You can know many things, but the wisdom of God is untouchable and absolutely incredible! You are presented with hundreds of choices every day. There will be difficult decisions that must be made in different seasons of your life. Having His wisdom and discernment will help you make decisions with confidence.

Spiritual insight and wisdom can only be found and learned through spending time with God. He is the source of *all* that you're searching for and *all* that you need.

Dear Lord,

Please give me Your wisdom in making this decision. Bring me clarity and Your peace so I know that I am listening to Your instructions and walking in Your will. Bless me with discernment when I am presented with challenging choices.

September 19

Let your roots grow down into Him, and let your lives be built on Him. Then your faith will grow strong in the truth you were taught, and you will overflow with thankfulness.
~Colossians 2:7

Weak or compromised roots of a plant lead to damage, collapse, and/or death of the plant. Similarly, if the roots we plant in Jesus Christ & His truth are unsteady or undependable, then our faith begins to dwindle and our spirit is bruised.

To plant and maintain strong, healthy roots in Christ, keep your eyes fixed on Him, never stop praying, saturate your mind with His word, and surround yourself with Godly people who are strong in their faith that can uplift you.

Dear Father,

I invite you into my heart, mind, and soul to plow up anything in me that weakens my roots in You and Your word. No matter how uncomfortable I feel, take out any habits, thoughts, dreams, and desires that don't allow roots to remain securely in place.

September 20

*He canceled the record of the charges against us
and took it away by nailing it to the cross.*
~Colossians 2:14

Jesus disarmed the spiritual rulers by his victory on the cross!

If you begin to feel that nothing or no person can ever forgive you, remember that your record is always clear in God's eyes. Ask Him for forgiveness and repent with a genuine heart. Even if you drifted far from Him, you will experience His beautiful mercy.

Dear Jesus,

I am sorry for venturing off Your path. I confess of all my sins and repent. Thank you for forgiving me and declaring me free of all charges. Help me to accept such a wonderful gift with humility.

September 21

Since you have been raised to new life with Christ,
set your sights on the realities of heaven,
where Christ sits in the place of honor at God's right hand.
~Colossians 3:1

Living here on Earth is temporary. Jesus has prepared a place for you at the right hand of his Father in heaven.

If you ever begin to feel unworthy, unloved, unforgiven, lonely, anxious, or afraid, <u>remember your identity in Christ</u>.

God's word is *perfect and true,* and He says that you are worthy, beautiful, loved, and forgiven. He is omnipresent and with you wherever you are, so you never need to feel lonely. Jesus is peace and hope, so when anxiety or fear come, whisper his name.

Dear Lord,

Direct my attention to heaven in all circumstances. Help me to really zero in on my true identity – who You say I am. Enhance my awareness of Your presence and keep my faith sound and resilient.

September 22

But now is the time to get rid of anger, rage, malicious behavior, slander, and dirty language.
~Colossians 3:9

Now is the time. No more excuses. Jesus' words are life-giving, encouraging, loving, thoughtful, helpful, intentional, and gentle. The great commission calls us to teach the Good News and be the hands and feet of Jesus. There is no way we can succeed at being a humble servant if anger, immoral behavior, and foul words are parts of our daily lives.

Let go of anger and bitterness. Eliminate slander and gossip. Clothe yourself in genuine mercy, kindness, humility, gentleness, patience, and of course, love.

Dear Lord,

I am tired of living in a state of anger, bitterness, and negativity. Father, work freely within me to transform me from the inside out.

September 23

Let the message about Christ, in all its richness,
fill your lives. Teach and counsel each other
with all the wisdom he gives. Sing psalms and hymns
and spiritual songs to God with thankful hearts.
~Colossians 3:16

Inviting Jesus into your heart and asking the Holy Spirit to guide you are the best choices you can make. His perfect, unending love will flow within and out of you so that you can love others better. His amazing peace that is simply indescribable will reside in you. His incredible strength is what helps you persevere during life's storms. Furthermore, you will be a light of hope to those in need and to the lost souls who do not know Jesus.

Dear Jesus,

I surrender to You. Soak my heart and control my mind. Please make me more attentive to your Holy Spirit so I am able to counsel others with God's wisdom.

September 24

*Devote yourselves to prayer with an alert mind
and a thankful heart.*
~Colossians 4:2

Intentionally devote private time for the Precious One who
deserves it more than anything or anyone else in the world!
Praying with an *alert mind* means to sit quietly in a place free
from all distractions. Praying with a *thankful heart* means to
thank God regardless of your current circumstance or feelings.
Praise Him anyway, even if it is hard.

One of Satan's main goals is to take your gaze off of God and
Truth. The enemy is a master manipulator and thrives on
stealing your joy and peace. He gladly throws distractions
your way to divert your attention off of your prayer time with
God. Do not give him the edge to do so. Stay focused on your
heavenly Father! He will surely bless you for remaining
faithful to Him during trying times.

Dear Lord,

*Please help me to focus on prayer and Your Presence wholeheartedly.
Teach me to know when Satan is trying to distract me and give me
courage to fight against him with scripture, prayer, and genuine
faith. Keep my mind alert and heart grateful.*

September 25

Let your conversation be gracious and attractive
so that you'll have the right response for everyone.
~Colossians 4:6

We have all been unsure of what to say before. We wondered if our words would be *right* or adequate. Will we respond the right way?

Jesus' mind and heart are unmatched, yet when we ask Him to give us the words to say, He will. If you are ever unsure of what someone needs to hear, simply invite the Holy Spirit to speak for you.

Dear Lord,

Thank you for giving me the privilege and honor to be your vessel here on earth. Please give me the exact words _____ needs to hear. Speak through me. I ask that they are uplifted and comforted through my words that come from You.

September 26

So you received the message with joy from the Holy Spirit in
spite of the severe suffering it brought you.
In this way, you imitated both us and the Lord.
~1 Thessalonians 1:6

Even though the Thessalonians suffered for accepting the
Good News, they still received *joy* because of their belief and
faith. God does not guarantee us a problem free life. In fact,
He tells us we will have trials and we will experience
suffering, but to *take heart* because Jesus has overcome the
world.

How is it possible to experience peace and joy during
adversity, pain, or misery? It is possible by staying connected
to Jesus Christ. His perfect peace and amazing joy are readily
available. <u>All you need to do is seek Him.</u>

Dear Jesus,

Thank you for sacrificing your life on the cross so that I may have
eternal life. Thank you for the precious gift of your Holy Spirit!
During times of suffering, please replace my sadness and doubt with
joy and confidence.

September 27

For we speak as messengers approved by God to be entrusted with the Good News. Our purpose is to please God, not people. He alone examines the motives of our hearts.
~1 Thessalonians 2:4

So many of us exert our energy into pleasing others. We judge ourselves, scrutinizing what we do or don't do, have or don't have, and how we look. We spend excess mental energy overanalyzing people and situations. And, we spend way too much time playing the comparison game.

Live a righteous life seeking His kingdom without judging or comparing yourself to others. Give up the habit of analyzing others' words or actions. Stop worrying about others' successes, blessings, or what they may do/say.

Our purpose is to live in God's will and to please Him above all. Knowing this takes off a great amount of pressure. *Relax.* You only have to live for one person - the One and only God Almighty! He asks that You please Him by sharing the Good News with others.

Dear Father,

Thank you for entrusting me with the Good News. Point out those in my life who You want me to share the gospel with, and fill me with confidence to do so. I pray that they hear Your truth and realize how deeply You love them.

September 28

So be on your guard, not asleep like the others.
Stay alert and be clear headed!
~1 Thessalonians 5:6

Satan is the father of lies. He knows exactly what will knock us off balance and crush our faith. He knows exactly how to stir up anxiety, fear, and doubt.

If you want to be able to quickly extinguish the enemy's nasty lies and ignore his mind tricks, then first, be on guard! Know when he is attacking. Second, always wear the armor of God so that you are adequately prepared. Third, remain clear headed by knowing Truth.

Dear God,

Keep me fully alert and on guard against Satan at all times. Please give me spiritual ears so I can easily distinguish when he whispers lies. Thank you for your constant protection and unfailing love.

September 29

*See that no one pays back evil for evil, but always
try to do good to each other and to all people.*
~1 Thessalonians 5:15

Instead of paying someone back with harsh words, forgive
them and treat them with kindness. Instead of taking revenge
with evil behavior, show them mercy and be generous with
love. Do your best to be respectful towards everyone,
including your enemies.

Dear God,

*I am sorry for my sinful thoughts and actions. I want to respond
with goodness, kindness, and gentleness towards everyone. Father, I
give you total control over my heart.*

September 30

Be thankful in all circumstances, for this is God's will for you
who belong to Christ Jesus.
~1 Thessalonians 5:18

Although you may not understand why that terrible tragedy
struck, unimaginable illness arose, or unsurmountable
problem came, be thankful.

Don't spend all your energy into trying to figure out *why*. God
has a purpose, and that is all you need to know. Your eyes
may be clouded with tears and ears clogged with
disheartening words, but understand that not a single tear is
ever wasted and that God will get you through it His way and
in His perfect time.

Dear God,

Thank you for this opportunity to trust you more. Thank you for
strengthening our relationship and solidifying my faith. I believe
You know what's best, so I trust You during the good and bad times.

October 1

Then the name of our Lord Jesus will be honored because of
the way you live, and you will be honored along with him.
This is all made possible because of the grace
of our God and Lord, Jesus Christ.
~2 Thessalonians 1:12

Ultimately, Jesus is glorified because of the lives of believers.
We honor him through the righteous ways we live.

Furthermore, we are honored *with* Him. How remarkable! Not
only is our Savior honored through our righteousness, but we
are as well. This is only possible because of His amazing
grace.

Dear Jesus

Thank you for the endless grace you bless me with every day. Reveal
to me ways in which I can bring more honor and glory to your name
with my actions.

October 2

*But the lord is faithful; He will strengthen you
and guard you from the evil one.
~2 Thessalonians 3:3*

People will let you down. A friend may prove untrustworthy. A coworker may double cross you. A family member can be deceitful or disloyal.

Well, it is impossible for the Lord our God to be unfaithful. He is our source of strength. He provides an unbreakable wall of protection against any kind of evil! He is completely trustworthy, loyal, and loving at all times.

Dear Father,

Thank you for being fully devoted to me. I know I can rely on You in all circumstances and at all times because of your faithfulness and love!

October 3

Oh, how generous and gracious our lord was! He filled me
with the faith and love that come from Christ Jesus.
~1 Timothy 1:14

Timothy accompanied Paul during Paul's ministry in
Ephesus. After some time, Timothy was given the task of
attending to false teachers and dilemmas in the church. Paul's
letters to Timothy guided him towards correcting behavior
and preventing false teachers from influencing Christians.

God's abundant love abides within you. Despite our sinful
nature, God graciously fills us with His unconditional love.
It's up to us to access it from deep within and put it to good
use.

Dear Father,

Thank you for your consistent, everlasting grace and love. Replace
every worry or doubt I have with absolute faith. Teach me how I can
model your grace, love, and faith to others.

October 4

All honor and glory to God forever and ever! He is the eternal king, the unseen one who never dies. He alone is God. Amen.
~1 Timothy 1:17

Be thankful for everything, including what seems to be insignificant to you. *Change your perspective* on frustrating situations, difficult relationships, and awful circumstances.

When you truly grasp the fact that God *works everything into a pattern for good for those who love him* and when you remain faithful to the Lord during trials, then thanksgiving and praise will flow from you even in the toughest of times because you <u>know with certainty</u> that God is the everlasting, all-powerful, perfect, righteous Lord and He has everything under control.

This steady faith and confidence in Him will leave no room for worry, fear, or doubt to take root in your mind.

Dear Lord,

You are King of kings! I give you <u>all</u> the glory and praise. Please grant me a heavenly perspective during challenging times. Comfort me with Your loving Presence and the reminder that You are in total control.

October 5

Cling to your faith in Christ, and keep your conscience clear.
For some people have deliberately violated their consciences;
as a result, their faith has been shipwrecked.
~1 Timothy 1:19

Disobeying the Lord by deliberately sinning will cast your faith away! Without faith and hope, one can fall into a pit of depression easier or become stuck in a harmful cycle.

Keep a tight grip on your faith at all times. Go to godly people who will pray for you, encourage you, and have faith for you when yours begins to weaken. You are not alone. Seek wise counsel from fellow Christians who have experienced what you are going through. Remain in prayer to your Father. He blesses those who seek Him and remain devoted to Him.

Dear God,

I never want to abandon my faith. Do not allow the enemy's lies to instill doubt, fear, or insecurity in me! I rebuke Satan's attempts at distracting me from You. I will remain in relationship with You so that my conscience stays pure and clear.

October 6

I urge you, first of all, to pray for all people. Ask God to help them; intercede on their behalf, and give thanks for them.
~1 Timothy 2:1

Notice that Paul *urges* (stresses the importance of) us to pray for *all people.*

He knew how easy it was to dismiss those who cause harm. He knew that those who manipulate, lie, mislead, and hurt us would certainly not be at the top of our prayer list. He knew that those who irritate us, push our buttons, and test our patience would not be who we desire to pray for.

Don't solely pray for yourself and loved ones. It is crucial to pray for those who are different from you and yes, even your enemies. They need prayer more than you realize. So, the next time you are with an annoying coworker, an impatient stranger in the grocery store, or someone causing harm, pray for them. Instead of judging them, bashing them, or gossiping about them or what they did, just pray that they see the light of Jesus and that they drift towards God's love. When God is at the center of one's heart, wicked behavior will not be present.

Dear Jesus,

Thank you for putting me in situations where I have the opportunity to pray for those who need it most. I ask that you please point out to me who I can specifically pray for today.

October 7

Since everything God created is good,
we should not reject any of it, but receive it with thanks.
~1 Timothy 4:4

Practice thanking your heavenly Father out loud for
everything: giving you another day of life, the rising sun, your
bed and home, and the shoes that protect your feet and
sweater that keeps you warm. Continuously thank Him for
everything and everyone in your life, whether you perceive it
to be positive or negative. Blessings follow after thanksgiving
and praise leave your lips.

God works in mysterious ways, giving us blessings in
disguise and bringing light from the darkness. It can be
impossible in our mind to see joy or feel peace during tragedy,
but remember that God is at work and He doesn't want you to
reject it or run from Him into sin and giving into temptation.

Receive it, and receive it with thanks. How do you receive
hardship like that? Only with the help of Jesus Christ, who is
omnipresent waiting for you to call on His name.

Dear God,

I know that everyone and everything You created, are creating, and
will create are made for good. Help me to refrain from rejecting any
of it and to instead receive and accept it as Your loving kindness.

October 8

*Physical training is good, but training for godliness is
much better, promising benefits in this life
and in the life to come!*
~1 Timothy 4:8

Training for anything takes dedication, determination, and
perseverance. Physical training is necessary and healthy for
you. Exercise is important for both your physical and
emotional health. You must practice consistently to see results
from working out. Athletes work constantly to strengthen
muscles and prepare for victory. Do not allow physical
training to override spiritual training.

Intentionally dedicate time to forming and strengthening an
intimate relationship with God. Do your best to live
righteously and remain faithful to Him so that you can enjoy
all of the blessings He has for you both here and in heaven!

Not only will the sovereign Lord answer your prayers and
bless you while on earth, but He gives you treasure in heaven!

Dear God,

*Please make training for spiritual battles and living a righteous life
priorities for me. Give me perseverance and motivation, and do not
let other desires distract me from training for godliness.*

October 9

After all, we brought nothing with us when we came into the world, and we can't take anything with us when we leave it.
~1 Timothy 6:7

Jesus tells us to give generously, help those in need, serve others joyfully, and treat everyone with love. Those are the things that matter on Earth – not how big your house is, how fancy your car is, or how lavish your possessions are. Clinging to what you physically have will not provide you with true peace or fulfill any void. There is only *One* to cling to – Jesus Christ.

This is also a wonderful reminder that God provides exactly what we need. Always. It may seem like we have nothing, but in fact we have everything because we have the Lord.

Dear God,

I live for You and desire to remain in Your will. Please do not let Satan deceive me into thinking material possessions, my career, or even relationships should be my main focus. You are my focus, Father. Return my gaze to You whenever it drifts.

October 10

Fight the good fight for the true faith.
Hold tightly to the eternal life to which God has called you,
which you have declared so well before many witnesses.
~1 Timothy 6:12

Not only did God love us so deeply that He sent Jesus to save us from death, but He wants us to sit next to Him in heaven! Praise God!

The least we can do is obey Him by fighting the good fight and teaching the Good News, saving as many lost people we can before our time on earth ends.

Dear Lord,

Thank you for giving me the privilege to share the Good News with others. Thank you for choosing me to be a vessel which guides people to Truth. Thank you for living in my heart and shining through me so that others see and experience Your love.

October 11

*Teach those who are rich in this world not to be proud and
not to trust in their money, which is so unreliable.
Their trust should be in God, who richly gives us
all we need for our enjoyment.
~1 Timothy 6:17*

How can so many wealthy and famous people be depressed?
They believe money and things lead to happiness. Greed and
pride take root and flourish. Frustration sets in because they
trust that their money and gifts will fill the void within and
make them happy. Sure, elegant gifts and fancy cars can
provide joy, but that joy is only temporary and never fully
satisfies.

Be humble and kind. Place your trust in Jesus because He is
undeniably the key to true happiness and peace. He gives you
everything you need and blesses you in abundance when You
follow Him.

Dear Father,

*Come into my heart and uproot all pride, greed, and selfishness. Do
not let me even entertain the thought that money and things lead to
happiness. Thank you for being the same yesterday, today, and
forever. I place my trust in You.*

October 12

*For God hasn't given us a spirit of fear and timidity,
but of power, love, and self-discipline.*
~2 Timothy 1:7

Worry, doubt, and fear are a waste of mental and emotional energy. Because God's word is flawless, His promises perfect, His character unchanging, His faithfulness and compassion unending, and His love for you unconditional, being anxious or afraid is absolutely unnecessary.

When you feel those anxious thoughts, doubts, or insecurities creeping up again, *relax*. God is with you and He gives you a spirit of strength and confidence. When you feel that uneasiness in your stomach or the panic that accompany your greatest fears, remind yourself that the Holy Spirit, which is *in you*, is a spirit of power and love: Jesus' perfect love casts out fear!

Dear Father,

When adversity strikes, chaos unfolds, or fear floods in, I will say "Thank you" and depend on You to help me through. Thank you for blessing me with a spirit of power, love, and self-discipline.

October 13

And now, he's made all of this plain to us by the appearing of Christ Jesus, our Savior. He broke the power of death and illuminated the way to life and immortality through the Good News.
~2 Timothy 1:10

There are many ways someone can "be in the dark." You can literally be in the pitch-black because of lack of power and light. You may be "in the dark" in the sense that your coworkers or family know something, but you were left out. You can also be in a dark pit of depression, anger, stress, or fear.

Being in darkness is not only frightening, but also dangerous. The enemy loves when we are in darkness and isolated, and he won't hesitate to take advantage of our vulnerability in that time. Jesus is our brilliant light who illuminates our path. His light cannot dim, flicker, or burn out. He is the way, the truth, the light. Halleluiah!

Dear Jesus,

I praise Your mighty name! Thank you for shining Your light in the darkness. Keep my eyes aware of Your light at all times and in every circumstance.

October 14

If we are unfaithful, He remains faithful,
for He can't deny who He is.
~2 Timothy 2:13

Our emotions fluctuate, our motives change, our sinful nature still transpires, and our faith wavers. God can be fully trusted because He is always faithful.

Sin and failures are just part of life. Confess of your sin and repent because no matter how unworthy or shameful you may feel or how terrible things appear, the Lord forgives. Every time, He forgives. His faithfulness and abundant mercy remain forever.

Dear Lord,

I am sorry for being unfaithful to You. I am sorry for allowing distractions to take over and not seek You first. Thank you for staying faithful to me in spite of my sins. Please ignite a fire in me to remain devoted to You.

October 15

But God's truth stands firm like a foundation stone with this inscription: "The Lord knows those who are His" and "All who belong to the Lord must turn away from evil."
~2 Timothy 2:19

The sturdiest building can still crumble. The strongest human is still susceptible to falling ill and weak.

The Bible is our reliable and secure groundwork for righteous living. Dive into God's word to root yourself firmly in the unbreakable foundation of God!

Dear Heavenly Father,

Please give me clarity and understanding as I read Your Truth. Bring to light whatever it is that You want me to know and learn. Provide confirmation and send me Your peace as I search for answers in Your Word.

October 16

Gently instruct those who oppose the truth. Perhaps God will change those people's hearts, and they will learn the truth.
~2 Timothy 2:25

Only God can soften, open, and transform someone's heart. Only He can transform someone by renewing their mind.

But, *you* have the privilege of sharing the gospel with others, teaching them God's Truth. Some listen joyfully, accepting and believing in it wholeheartedly. Others may be skeptical.

Be patient with them. Speak softly and calmly. Teach them God's promises, His instructions, and the Truth in love. Do not waste any opportunity to talk about God's goodness, His amazing miracles, and His profound, unconditional love.

Dear Lord,

Point out to me who You would like me to teach Your word to. Lord, soften his/her heart and give him/her an open mind so Your promises, instructions, and truth enter his/her heart effortlessly.

October 17

*All scripture is inspired by God and is useful to teach us what
is true and to make us realize what is wrong in our lives.
It corrects us when we're wrong and teaches us
to do what is right.*
~2 Timothy 3:16

Our curious minds are full of questions. We yearn to find
answers and solutions to problems.

Scripture teaches us how to treat others and what is
important. The Bible is our roadmap. God explains our true
identity and that heaven is our home. Jesus' character is
beautifully modeled through His deep compassion. The Holy
Spirit helps us recognize our sin and guides us to repentance.
The more aware of the Holy Spirit you become, the easier it
will be to really hear what the Lord is saying and to
confidently make choices God wants you to make.

God corrects us out of pure love. Do not run from pain or hide
from fear. Do not fall into despair. Allow the situation to train
you. God is indeed working. Intentionally be on the lookout
for His hand in your life.

Dear Father,

*Thank you for the gift of Your Holy Spirit who connects me to Your
Presence and helps me recognize Your will and plans for my life. I
appreciate Your correction. Help me submit everything to You.
Please reveal how You are working in my life.*

October 18

But you should keep a clear mind in every situation.
Don't be afraid of suffering for the Lord.
Work at telling others the Good News,
and fully carry out the ministry God has given you.
~2 Timothy 4:5

God has called all of His children to spread the Good News.
There is no reason to be shy, nervous, or fearful to talk about
God or share your testimony. If others ridicule or discourage
you, take heart. God is proud of you and loves you more than
you can comprehend.

Dear Lord,

*Please give me enthusiasm as I carry out the ministry You have
given me of sharing the gospel with others. I will not fear in
affliction or suffering because You are with me – protecting,
comforting, and guiding me. Thank you Father!*

October 19

*Yes, the Lord will deliver me from every evil attack and will
bring me safely into His heavenly kingdom.
All glory to God forever and ever. Amen!*
~2 Timothy 4:18

Jesus tells us we will face trials and suffering in this corrupted
world. Understand that your sorrow and heartache are never
wasted. He frees you from all evil because you are His child,
His treasured possession that He has set apart.

Never stop praying and do not lose faith during your
suffering. Cling to Jesus, your *hope*.

Dear Lord,

*Thank you for being my secure fortress in whom I can trust
completely to keep me safe from evil. I may not understand why
certain afflictions come my way, but I trust that You will bring good
from it.*

October 20

And you yourself must be an example to them by doing good works of every kind. Let everything you do reflect the integrity and seriousness of your teaching.
~Titus 2:7

Paul wrote to Titus asking him to encourage both the men and women in the church to live wisely by showing love, patience, faith, and forgiveness. Paul emphasized the importance of the church leaders teaching the truth and setting the example for others.

Integrity is how you act when no one is watching. Be honorable, respectful, and wise whether you have an audience or not. Set a positive and commendable example to everyone including your family, friends, co-workers, and strangers so that they can catch a glimpse of Jesus' light.

Dear God,

Thank you for being the ultimate example of living with integrity. Reveal to me how I can act and speak more lovingly and righteously. I invite you to transform anything necessary within me so that I can shine Your light brighter!

October 21

And we are instructed to turn from godless living and sinful pleasures. We should live in this evil world with wisdom, righteousness, and devotion to God.
~Titus 2:12

Notice this requires action - *turn from*. When you know certain "friends" are negatively influencing you and hindering your relationship with the Lord, do not hang out with them.

When sinful desires and temptations arise, turn around and walk the opposite way. Look up to God.

Dear God,

Please give me tenacious boldness to immediately turn from my sinful pleasures. When I am tempted, give me absolute confidence and strength to deny the temptation. Guide me along the path of righteousness.

October 22

*He gave His life to free us from every kind of sin, to cleanse us,
and to make us His very own people, totally committed
to doing good deeds.*
~Titus 2:14

How polluted our lives would be without Jesus' death and
resurrection. He made us as white as snow!

Do not let your past mistakes and sins paralyze you. Do not
allow Satan's lies to be the thoughts you pay attention to. You
are *worthy*. You are *loved*. You are *forgiven*. God bestows
endless grace and mercy upon you no matter how many times
you sin or how far you drift from him. Relax. When you
repent, you are *freed from every chain and burden!* You are
forgiven of *all sin*.

Dear Lord,

*Thank you for loving me in my brokenness. I confess all sins to you.
Reveal the sins I am unconscious of so that I can surrender those to
you and repent from them as well. Thank you for your endless
forgiveness, mercy, and grace.*

October 23

*And I am praying that you will put into action
the generosity that comes from your faith as you understand
and experience all the good things we have in Christ.*
~Philemon 1:6

Paul is hinting here for us to be gracious because of the grace
God extends to us.

When your brain truly registers God's goodness, praise and
thanksgiving will follow naturally. Giving will become
straightforward because of your strong faith in Christ, which
you build when you experience His blessings and goodness.

Dear Jesus,

*I am forever grateful for your astounding grace. Help me to be
generous with grace and forgiveness to everyone. Give me extra
strength to do so with my enemies.*

October 24

The Son radiates God's own glory and expresses the very character of God, and He sustains everything by the mighty power of His command. When He had cleansed us from our sins, He sat down in the place of honor at the right hand of the majestic God in heaven.
~Hebrews 1:3

Jesus is greater than anything you can fathom. By simply whispering Jesus' precious name when you feel lonely, scared, or exhausted, His Presence will begin to calm you as His peace enters your body through the Holy Spirit.

Jesus is our prime example of God's character: demonstrating genuine compassion and love towards everyone, praying to His Father continually, extending forgiveness and grace towards all, and teaching the Truth in love.

Dear God,

Thank you for sending Your one and only Son to be my Savior and to purify me of all sin. Please make me more sensitive to the Holy Spirit's voice. Help me to obey immediately even when I am confused, uncomfortable, or afraid.

October 25

So, we must listen very carefully to the truth we have heard,
or we may drift away from it.
~Hebrews 2:1

It's not enough to inattentively listen to your pastor's message or read the Bible quickly. You must *listen carefully* to God's promises and instructions so that you can understand and apply them. Furthermore, you must *listen carefully* to ensure you do not drift from His Truth.

Dear Lord,

Please keep the voices and clamor of the world from being what I focus on listening to. My desire is to hear Your voice, Your promises, Your instructions, and Your will, so I ask that You remove anything that blocks me from hearing You. Thank you Father!

October 26

*And, God confirmed the message by giving signs and wonders
and various miracles and gifts of the Holy Spirit
whenever he chose.*
~Hebrews 2:1

The book of Hebrews provides true stories of the blessings
and miracles that those who remained faithful to God
received. We can confidently hope in Jesus and surely trust
God's promises.

The saying "I'll believe it when I see it" is common. Even
though we don't physically see God, we can believe in Him by
experiencing His powerful presence, seeing His wonders, and
witnessing His incredible miracles. These signs and wonders
can be a gorgeous sunset or exquisite landform. They can also
be circumstances that work out ever so perfectly that it seems
like an amazing coincidence, but that is God's work in action!

The Lord performs miracles every day like wiping away a
terminal illness in an instant, providing a solution for an
impossible problem, and giving immediate freedom to chains
of bondage. And, He does all this with great ease because He
is our mighty God! Intentionally look for the Father's signs,
wonders, and miracles, and *you will see them!*

Dear Lord,

*I do not want to miss out on any of Your amazing miracles, signs,
and wonders. Please make me more aware of Your Presence. Give me
the courage to share Your power and glory with others.*

October 27

So now Jesus and the ones He makes holy have the same Father. That's why Jesus is not ashamed to call them his brothers and sisters.
~Hebrews 2:11

Because Jesus made us holy, we belong to God, the Father of all creation. It seems unreal that Jesus, who is perfect love and has unmatched power, is our brother, friend, High Priest, and Savior.

Although we maintain a sinful nature, Jesus is never tired of us or ashamed of us. He will never let us down. He generously gives blessings, endless love, and mercy.

Dear Jesus,

Thank you for your holy sanctification and unconditional love. Show me how I can love my brothers and sisters better. Bring to light any area within my character that needs to be more gentle, loving, and hospitable. Transform my heart to be more like yours.

October 28

For the word of God is alive and powerful.
It's sharper than the sharpest two-edged sword,
cutting between soul and spirit, between joint and marrow.
It exposes our innermost thoughts and desires.
~Hebrews 4:12

Let your mind, body, and spirit unwind in God's Presence.
Release everything into His care, for He can effortlessly carry
all the burdens of everyone on the planet. The same God who
made the lame walk, made the blind see, instantly healed
diseases, and created mankind with the breath from his
nostrils and dirt from the ground is the *exact same God* we
worship today! God is very much alive and powerful.

Dear Lord,

*As I read Your Word, give me a clear understanding of its power
and significance. Bring to light anything within my heart or mind
that is ungodly, and help me to change. Please keep Truth at the
forefront of my mind and help me to fight spiritual battles with
scripture accurately and carefully.*

October 29

In this way, God qualified him as a perfect High Priest,
and he became the source of eternal salvation
for all those who obey him.
~Hebrews 5:9

Jesus was qualified to be God's High Priest because of His suffering. Jesus submitted to God and His will even though that involved great anguish and discomfort.

When you know you are in God's will, you can have a sense of peace even in the midst of the heartbreak and agony. Troubles are not meaningless.

Dear Father,

As Jesus submitted to your will, I submit as well. I know you have my best interest in mind and that all things will work according to your plan and timing. Please give me peace during times of confusion, discomfort, anxiety, and stress.

October 30

So let us stop going over the basic teachings about Christ again and again. Let us go on instead and become more mature in our understanding. Surely we don't need to start again with the fundamental importance of repenting from evil deeds and placing our faith in God.
~Hebrews 6:1

Concentrate on *understanding* scripture. Study Bibles are excellent because they provide context, definitions, maps and pictures, and more to help you grasp what is happening. Join a life group or Bible study to enhance your knowledge of the Almighty.

You can't know what you don't know. Make knowing God and maintaining a personal relationship with Him your priority. You will be blessed indeed.

Dear Father,

You are far from basic and ordinary! Help me to dive deep into Your word with enhanced focus so I can learn from Your instructions and have solid faith. Show me how I can apply your truth in my personal life and how I can use your instructions to help others as well.

October 31

This hope is a strong and trustworthy anchor for our souls.
It leads us through the curtain into God's inner sanctuary.
~Hebrews 6:19

Boat anchors keep the boat securely in place. In the same way, if you want to stay securely tied to God, keep your hope in Him alive at all times. Trust in Him. Holding onto His promises is your best protection against whatever comes your way!

If you're waiting for a miracle or prayer to be answered, be patient. Keep your eyes fixed on Jesus, be persistent with prayer, and do not lift the anchor of hope. The waiting is preparing you for when the answer and/or blessing arrives.

Dear Father,

Please infuse me with steady, unbreakable faith. Revitalize my strength so I do not let go of Hope, the anchor of my soul. Although I am weak, You are strong and I trust you. Thank you for this opportunity to nourish my spirit and fortify my hope in You.

November 1

And without question, the person who has the power to give a blessing is greater than the one who's blessed.
~Hebrews 7:7

If we aren't careful, greed, selfishness, and/or envy can take control of our minds. Rather than focusing on just receiving blessings, think of how you can bless someone else.

Try being selfless today by generously giving others your time, attention, and love. Help the elderly woman with her groceries. Smile at the store associates. When you notice your neighbor struggling in the yard, offer assistance.

Whoever is in need, *be a blessing* to them without hesitating. You will surely be blessed, but more importantly, the person will see the Light of the World – Jesus – shining through your kind deeds.

Dear Father,

Thank you for blessing me so that I can bless others. Show me who I can bless today and tell me how I can bless them. May they see the light of Jesus shine through me and feel Your loving presence.

November 2

*He is the kind of high priest we need because he is holy and
blameless, unstained by sin. He has been set apart
from sinners and has been given the highest
place of honor in heaven.*
~Hebrews 7:26

Praise God for sending a holy priest! His son Jesus is seated in
heaven at the highest place of honor. In spite of all our sin, He
calls us to sit next to Him in heaven! This alone is enough
reason for you to praise Him at *all times*, through the good and
the bad, through smooth sailing and rough patches, through
the ups and downs of life, and through seasons of confidence
and peace as well as seasons of fear and confusion.

Our holy, blameless, perfect Lord is exactly what we need.

Dear Jesus,

*You are superior to all priests because of your holiness. Thank you
for sanctifying me and inviting me to sit next to you in heaven. That
is the highest honor anyone can ever receive, so thank you for loving
me that much.*

November 3

But now Jesus, our High Priest, has been given a ministry
that is far superior to the old priesthood, for he is the one
who mediates for us a far better covenant with God,
based on better promises.
~Hebrews 8:6

A mediator is someone who helps two parties come to an agreement. When Jesus sacrificed His life for ours, that established the covenant relationship between us and the Father. This new covenant is based on better promises.

Jesus prays to the Father on our behalf, too. When we don't have the words to say, Jesus relays our emotions and needs to God himself.

Dear Jesus,

Thank you for being the best mediator possible. I know that you speak to our Father on my behalf, so help me to surrender everything to You in complete trust.

November 4

*For God's will was for us to be made holy by the sacrifice
of the body of Jesus Christ, once for all time.
~Hebrews 10:10*

When Jesus died on the cross, our sins were washed away for
all time.

Going to church and performing good deeds doesn't result in
eternal salvation. Eternal salvation belongs to **anyone who
believes** (*believes* in God, *believes* in His Son Jesus, and *believes*
in Jesus' crucifixion and resurrection) and who **accepts the
gift of salvation**.

God's will is for us to be holy and pure. Praise Him forever
because we have been sanctified through the death and
resurrection of Jesus Christ. He has chosen us and set us apart.

Dear Lord,

*Thank you for the ultimate gift of eternal salvation. I am forever
grateful and feel blessed beyond measure that you chose me to be
your child, set apart for your glory. Please humble my heart. May
praise, honor, and glory for you flow from my lips every day.*

November 5

Let us hold tightly without wavering to the hope we affirm,
for God can be trusted to keep his promise.
~Hebrews 10:23

When things are going great, it can be easy to loosen your grip
on the Lord. You don't feel that you need to hold onto His
word since currently everything is going well in your life. You
don't feel hopeless, so there seems to be no need to cling to
hope. This is precisely when you should tightly grasp onto
God and His word.

When stress or fear overwhelm you, a tragedy strikes, and/or
chaos is all around, it can be easy to let go of hope because it
may seem like victory or freedom is impossible. This is exactly
when you must hold onto hope, the anchor of your soul.

So, you see, it is crucial to *always* hold onto the hope you have
in Jesus, and to hold onto it tightly. Don't ever allow a
circumstance, person, or the enemy to influence you to loosen
your grip on it.

Dear Jesus,

You are my hope! Remind me to keep holding onto You & God's
promises during all seasons of my life. Use me to instill hope into
those who have lost it.

November 6

*Let us think of ways to motivate one another
to acts of love and good works.
~Hebrews 10:24*

No one wants to be left out in the cold, made fun of, discouraged, or treated poorly. Switch from seeing the negative in others to seeing their strengths and gifts.

Everyone was uniquely created by God. He has given each of us a special purpose. Strive for unity and peace. Propel each other towards success! Help one another reach goals. Serve, give, and help those in need.

Dear God,

I ask that the body of believers unite together peacefully to make the world a better place by teaching the Good News, being the hands & feet of Jesus, and showing love to everyone. Help us see others how You see them. Give us enthusiasm and determination to motivate one another through love!

November 7

Patient endurance is what you need now,
so that you will continue to do God's will.
Then, you will receive all that He has promised.
~Hebrews 10:36

Fatigue will come. Exhaustion will set in. Fear and doubt are natural human responses to uncertainties. What is important is that you do not allow exhaustion, fear, or defeat to cause you to quit! Whether you are in a dry season, a time of waiting on Him to answer a prayer, in a stressful situation, suffering deep pain, or going through any other type of affliction, pray for *patient endurance* to get you through.

Keep your eyes fixed on God and remain faithful to Him. Pray continually and trust Him. *Then,* you will receive all that He has promised.

Dear Lord,

Please maintain my stamina and perseverance throughout my entire race. Do not let Satan distract me from obeying Your will. Keep my eyes fixed upon you at all times.

November 8

Faith shows the reality of what we hope for;
it's the evidence of things we can't see.
~Hebrews 11:1

Lawyers present physical evidence on behalf of their client. The FBI and police use proof in their investigations and arrests. We prove our points by giving evidence and plausible reasons for arguments.

The hopes and dreams formed in our minds are invisible, but the evidence for their reality is our faith.

We believe in the air we breathe even though we do not see it. Christians who have accepted Jesus into their hearts as their Lord and Savior believe that He died on the cross and rose from the dead three days later, even though they didn't *see* it with their own eyes. They believe in God because they have felt His presence and have seen His miracles, signs, and wonders.

Just because you cannot see something does not mean it is not real. Faith is complete confidence in something that is unseen.

Dear God,

I believe in You! Although I do not see every detail, I will step out in faith, trusting You. I rebuke all of the enemy's attempts to diminish my faith and hope in you.

November 9

We do this by keeping our eyes on Jesus, the champion who initiates and perfects our faith. Because of the joy awaiting him, he endured the cross, disregarding its shame. Now, he is seated in the place of honor beside God's throne.
~Hebrews 12:2

How do you strip off every weight, especially sin, that is slowing you down? Steady your gaze on Jesus Christ, the champion of faith.

Jesus was able to endure great suffering on the cross and die because He knew that he was going to be with his Father in heaven. We can endure hardships and suffering by staying close to Jesus because He is the one who *initiates and perfects our faith.*

Dear Father,

Thank you for Your son Jesus Christ. Please redirect my eyes back to Jesus when they venture away. When utter darkness surrounds me and my faith is depleting, please illuminate your Light even brighter and fill me with faith so that I can get through.

November 10

Have you forgotten the encouraging words God spoke to you as his children? He said, "My child, don't make light of the Lord's discipline, and don't give up when he corrects you."
~Hebrews 12:5

Discipline is necessary for safety and growth. It is both counterproductive and unwise to ignore discipline that is meant to keep you safe, teach you, help you, and strengthen you. Although it may not feel good in the moment, do not reject it.

It is paramount to accept the Lord's discipline and heed to it. Why? Because He knows you better than you know yourself and holds the entire world in His hands. Why would you disregard the all-knowing, all-powerful God who is the definition of wisdom? He is in control.

Dear Lord,

I know that You are for me, so thank you for your good discipline. I trust that it is meant to enhance my character. Please help me listen to Your loving voice and obey Your perfect instructions even when I feel like going my own way.

November 11

Since we are receiving a kingdom that's unshakable,
let us be thankful and please God by worshiping Him
with holy fear and awe.
~Hebrews 12:28

When you comprehend the fact that despite all your sins and wrongdoings God gave you an unshakable, magnificent eternity in heaven, you will surely worship Him with great respect.

Be thankful that God <u>generously</u> gives grace, mercy, and forgiveness each time you fall short. Show Him how grateful you are by worshiping Him in deep reverence and awe.

Dear God,

Thank you for freely giving me everlasting life and letting me spend eternity in your marvelous kingdom. Thank you for your constant overflowing grace and unending forgiveness. I worship Your holy name.

November 12

Don't love money; be satisfied with what you have. For God
said, "I'll never fail you. I'll never abandon you."
~Hebrews 13:5

When you walk trustingly with God, you have very little time
to be concerned about finances because you *know* that He will
provide you with exactly what you need and when. Why
would you even consider falling in love with money, a
material possession that you can't take with you to heaven
anyway?

Be content with what you have. Love the One who is always
with you!

Dear Lord,

Thank you for your steady companionship. Do not let me even begin
to become attached to money. Give me complete satisfaction and true
contentment with exactly what I have in the present moment. I know
that You fulfill my every need.

November 13

Jesus Christ is the same yesterday, today, and forever.
~Hebrews 13:8

People change their minds, actions, and attitudes. Throughout our lives, we may shift careers or transition to a new home. Modifications and transformations are common, but it is impossible for our Savior to change. This fact should send peace into your soul because you can <u>know without a doubt</u> that your Lord remains *perfect, faithful, and in control.*

Do everything in dependence of God. He gave us free will, but <u>we must use our freedom wisely</u> by seeking His guidance and relying on Him.

Mediate on His promises, remember His gracious blessings, and watch His breathtaking miracles unfold!

Dear Jesus,

Thank you for being 100% reliable in all circumstances and at all times. When my weakness is exposed or when others fail me, You are always there showering me with Your love, peace, grace, and forgiveness. Help me to never forget my dependence on You.

November 14

*Therefore, let us offer through Jesus a continual sacrifice
of praise to God, proclaiming our allegiance to His name.*
~Hebrews 13:15

The key words here are *continual sacrifice of praise.*

Sacrifice means to give up or to offer something. Give Jesus
your praise every day, regardless of your current situation.
Whether you are feeling on top of the world or feelings as
though the endless attacks are crushing you, praise Him.
Whether you are succeeding or failing, praise Him. Whether
things in your life are going smoothly or everything seems to
be spinning out of control, praise Him.

Jesus paid the ultimate sacrifice. He forgives our
transgressions and cleanses us completely every time we sin.
He fills us with inexplainable peace and showers us with
unconditional love. Therefore, He is most deserving of our
praise – in all circumstances.

Dear Jesus,

*Thank you for sacrificing your life for mine. Show me what I need to
sacrifice in my own life. Help me praise you during trials and
tragedies, and when I am hurting. I lift up your name, for You are
my Lord!*

November 15

Dear brothers and sisters, when troubles of any kind come your way, consider it an opportunity for great joy.
~James 1:2

Our strength and endurance grow when our faith is tested during times of trouble. Relax. Trust. Press on.

When hardship comes, Jesus does not want us to run away in fear, lash out in anger, or let anxiety take over. Rather, He asks that we respond with joy. You don't have to be happy you are full of stress, glad for the current chaos, or delighted for experiencing tragedies and pain. *But,* consider that trying time an <u>opportunity</u> *for great joy* because those difficulties, the heartache, and the pain are ingredients for God's miracles.

The darkness, challenges, and hurt are precisely the times when God shows up! His glory shines and His power is demonstrated like you've never seen.

Dear God,

Although I do not always understand why I go through certain troubles, I know that everything You allow is ultimately for Your good and perfect will, so thank you for this opportunity for joy! Father, please help me accept adversity with a positive attitude and motivate me to seek You during the struggle. Make me more aware of Your Presence and goodness.

November 16

Understand this my dear brothers and sisters:
You must all be quick to listen, slow to speak,
and slow to get angry.
~James 1:19

Jesus' ears are always alert to our cries, requests, and thanksgiving.

Sometimes His answers are fast, yet other times He responds slowly. He gently communicates with us.

Jesus never becomes outraged, even if we intentionally choose the wrong path over and over again. He never yells at us for falling into the deepest pit of sin.

We are called to love others as Jesus loves us. So, listen to others instead of interrupting, let others speak first instead of rushing to get your word in, and calm down when your nerves are pressed.

Dear Lord,

Thank you for listening to every plea, request, idea, dream, and cry that I lay before you! Thank you for taking your time to respond to me. I know you are doing so for my benefit. Thank you for being so patient with me. Please give me more patience, gentleness, and self-control.

November 17

For if you listen to the word and don't obey,
it's like glancing at your face in a mirror.
~James 1:23

Every instruction God gives is both important and purposeful.
He keeps every single one of His perfect promises. His
unfailing love and faithfulness are incomparable.

Blessings come to those who do their best to obey the Lord's
teaching and direction.

Be intentional about applying God's instructions in your life,
and ask Him how you can incorporate scripture in your
personal relationships with others.

Dear God,

Thank you for Your word! Please give me understanding as I read it.
Make my ears sensitive to the Holy Spirit's advice and direction.
Open my eyes so I'm able to see how intricately You are working in
my life and in the lives of those around me.

November 18

Just as the body is dead without breath,
so also faith is dead without good works.
~James 2:26

The body cannot live without breath. Similarly, faith cannot live without action. Simply believing in someone or something is not adequate. Genuine faith requires action. This may mean getting out of your comfort zone, leaving certain things or people behind, changing a habit, and more.

The enemy wants to cripple your faith! Stand firm in God's presence, meditating on Truth. Stay in community with your brothers and sisters in Christ who will have faith for you when yours runs low.

Dear Lord,

Your faithfulness astounds me. Please revitalize my faith every day. I believe in You and trust in Your sovereignty. Give me the boldness and tenacity to defend my faith! Help me to confidently stand up against Satan's attacks of fear and doubt.

November 19

And even when you ask, you don't get it because your motives are all wrong – you want only what will give you pleasure.
~James 4:3

We have all knocked on a door that would not open or sought something without finding it. We have all prayed to God for a specific request that wasn't fulfilled, at least not in the way we desired or in the timeframe we wished.

It's time to stop and think what your motives are behind that request. If your heart is selfish, impure, or not genuine, then why do you continue thinking you will receive what you want? God searches the whole earth for honest hearts.

Now, even if your heart is genuine and your request is "reasonable," God may not answer *because His plan is much greater* than you can ever dream of. Furthermore, He may very well answer, but you do not realize this because you are looking for *your answer* rather than His. God works in mysterious ways. To be attuned to how He works, you need to have an intimate relationship with Him.

Dear Father,

Thank you for guiding me in Truth. Examine my motives. Whatever displeases you, take it away. Transform my mind and purify my heart so that my motives please You. I submit my entire being to You and desire to live in Your will because I know that is the safest place to be.

November 20

Are any of you suffering hardships? You should pray.
Are any of you unhappy? You should sing praises.
~James 5:13

Complaining about problems to others won't solve it or add relief. Instead of focusing on the negatives, downfalls, and personal sufferings during a trial, go to the One who can literally pull you out of that situation in an instant! He may work immediately, but if not, *He will give you endurance and help you overcome it.* PRAY. Pour out your thoughts and feelings to Jesus.

Sulking in misery won't cure your sadness. Instead of glooming over your situation or falling into depression, *sing praises to Jesus.* Remember, He is the source of your joy.

Surrender to God's will and trust that He will bring beauty out of the affliction. He is waiting for your call – prayer and praise!

Dear Lord,

When disaster strikes, I will thank You for the opportunity to trust You more. I praise Your mighty name because it is You who turns my sorrow into joy, helps me overcome obstacles, and gives me victory.

November 21

You were cleansed from your sins when you obeyed the truth, so now you must show sincere love to each other as brothers and sisters. Love each other deeply with all your heart.
~1 Peter 1:22

Forgive sincerely and love *deeply*.

When Satan invades your mind, forgiveness, grace, and love are the last things on your mind. When God is truly in your heart, forgiveness, grace, and love become natural responses, even in conflict and turmoil. Replace anger with grace and substitute bitterness with kindness.

Dear Jesus,

Thank you for modeling how you want me to love others. Please help me to show genuine love to my family, friends, coworkers, and especially those who are difficult to love.

November 22

*And you are living stones that God is building
into His spiritual temple. What's more, you are His holy
priests. Through the mediation of Jesus Christ,
you offer spiritual sacrifices that please God.*
~1 Peter 2:5

Puzzles, cars and planes, and buildings are all made of many
smaller parts that make up the entire system. Each part is not
only necessary to make the whole come together, but critical.
When one part fails or breaks, it affects the whole - becoming
damaged and/or nonfunctional.

The Christian community is God's spiritual temple built on
the foundation of Jesus. How incredible that the Lord
Almighty calls us His holy priests! Scripture says *through the
mediation of Jesus, you offer spiritual sacrifices that please God.*
Jesus intervenes on our behalf and talks to the Father for us
when we are in dire need for Him.

Dear Father,

*Thank you for choosing me as one of Your holy priests. Teach me
what this means and help me apply it so I can help others come to
know You more. Reveal to me what I must sacrifice to please You. I
am tired of living life my own way. I strongly desire to know and
live out Your will alone.*

November 23

But you are not like that, for you are a chosen people. You are
royal priests, a holy nation, God's very own possession.
As a result, you can show others the goodness of God, for He
called you out of the darkness into His wonderful light.
~1 Peter 2:9

Because of the fact that God made you a royal priest and has
claimed you as His own, you are able to show others His
goodness. Your testimonies are especially powerful. Beautiful
hope floods into others' hearts when they hear about how the
Lord helped you through darkness or see how He performed
a miracle. Don't ever grow weary of expressing how great
God is!

Dear Lord,

You are a good, good Father. Even when I am lost, frustrated,
stressed, anxious, afraid, or confused, I can rest because I know that
when I am in Your Presence, darkness and fear flee. Show me how I
can express Your goodness to others every day and give me the
courage to boldly share my testimonies. Open their hearts, minds,
eyes, and ears to be receptive to my testimonies and Your loving
presence.

November 24

For you are free, yet you are God's slaves,
so do not use your freedom as an excuse to do evil.
~1 Peter 2:16

It's God's will that we live honorable lives, respecting everyone and loving the family of believers. God forgives each time we repent and pray the prayer of salvation, but that doesn't mean we should abuse our freedom by intentionally giving into temptation or purposely sinning and then asking for His forgiveness.

You know right from wrong. You know how to respect and honor your heavenly Father. Don't make excuses.

Dear Lord,

I am very grateful that You are my Master who has given me freedom. Please do not allow my free will to become an excuse to disobey or sin. When the actions of my brothers and sisters in Christ do not align with Your instructions, help me reveal Your Truth in love to them.

November 25

Once you were like sheep who wandered away. But now, you've turned to your Shepherd, the Guardian of your souls.
~1 Peter 2:25

Focusing on people, your current situation, and/or Satan's lies can quickly and easily lead you astray. Instead, gaze towards Jesus. He guides you precisely where you should be.

When your attention is on Jesus, you will overcome the obstacle and be freed from Satan's lies that chain you up before you know it! *Trust and obedience* are what get you through these tough times.

Dear Jesus,

Thank you for being my faithful guardian and for shepherding me where You want me to be. If I ever become distracted and wander from Your pasture, please make me aware immediately and guide me back. Help me to guide others to You.

November 26

Don't be concerned about the outward beauty of fancy hairstyles, expensive jewelry, or beautiful clothes.
~1 Peter 3:3

Society and culture today express so much emphasis on dazzling our appearance.

Don't be concerned about how you physically look. Greediness for lavish material possessions and the comparison game are terrible traps to be stuck in. They sprout bitterness, selfishness, and pride within your heart.

What is most important is to clothe yourself in loving kindness, gentleness, patience, and humility. Be concerned about your heart, character, and motives.

Dear God,

Thank you for loving me exactly how I am. Do not allow me to exert energy into my outward appearance. Instead, keep my focus on maintaining a pure heart and staying humble.

November 27

Do not repay evil for evil.
Do not retaliate with insults when people insult you.
Instead, pay them back with a blessing.
~1 Peter 3:9

Pause before responding. It is unwise to act immediately when emotions are intense. When someone backstabs you, attacks you with hurtful words, or does something terrible, instead of seeking revenge or lashing back with insults, *pay them back with kindness and a blessing.* Furthermore, pray for him/her.

Dear Father,

Thank you for responding to me with patience and love when I sin. Help me respond this way as well. Lord, I need You in every aspect of my life, and especially in this area. Help me forgive those who hurt me and my loved ones. Help me pay them back with kindness and blessings. Lord I need you because I cannot do this without Your help.

November 28

But even if you suffer for doing what's right,
God will reward you for it.
So don't worry or be afraid of their threats.
~1 Peter 3:14

Worrying when you obey God is meaningless. Obeying Him is absolutely merited. It doesn't matter if the entire world is against you or trying to discourage you. If God leads you somewhere and/or tells you to do something, obey without hesitation. Without fear. Without doubt. Without worry!

Obeying the Lord is <u>always right</u>, and although this may mean that you will undergo challenges or pain, <u>stay the course</u> because God's rewards and blessings are right around the corner. Do not be afraid of what anyone says. Do not allow Satan's schemes and lies to intimidate you.

With God, you are victorious.

Dear Father,

Thank you for the generous blessings You shower upon me. I know that obeying Your instructions may lead to difficulties, so help me endure with a positive mindset focused on Your love. Replace any worry or fear with confidence and courage.

November 29

*Most important of all, continue to show deep love for each
other, for love covers a multitude of sins.*
~1 Peter 4:8

Peter urges Christians to live for God through serving Him
and others, being genuine and persistent with prayer, and
most importantly *continue to show deep love.* Peter suggests that
love masks sins committed against us and covers our sins
because <u>love reflects our relationship with Jesus.</u>

Dear Lord,

*Thank you for loving me in my brokenness and sin. Thank you for
continuing to love me when I disobey Your Word, fall short, or am
unloving to others. Please help me to deeply love people in their
brokenness.*

November 30

Dear friends, do not be surprised at the fiery trials you're going through as if something strange were happening to you.
~1 Peter 4:12

Don't be startled when something unexpected ruins your whole day. Don't be overwhelmed when a "perfect" relationship or friendship falls apart. Don't be perplexed when things do not go according to your plan.

Nothing catches God off guard. He knows exactly what is happening.

We should actually be *glad* for problems and times of distress! When God gives us difficulties, He fully equips us to handle them and/or get through them. Life's storms are temporary. Both during the storm and after, His power and glory are at work.

Dear God,

Although this is difficult, I thank you for this attack. I know that You will never allow evil to be victorious. I ask that You give me the strength to press on and the faith to totally trust in You. Make my automatic response to trials be gratitude and trust instead of rage and anxiety.

December 1

Give all your worries and cares to God,
for He cares about you.
~1 Peter 5:7

Release every single worry to the Lord. Give each burden that's weighing you down to Him.

Satan wants you clinging to worry because that leads to a vicious cycle of doubt, anxiety, and fear. Believing his lies and succumbing to fear is precisely where he wants you. Refuse to give him a foothold in your life by casting all your worries and cares to God, your Father who is *for you.*

Dear Heavenly Father,

Help me recognize every lie from the enemy and rebuke it immediately. Lord, I give you every anxious thought that crosses my mind and every burden that weighs me down. Thank you for Your profound love for me!

December 2

Stay alert! Watch out for your great enemy, the devil.
He prowls around like a roaring lion,
looking for someone to devour.
~1 Peter 5:8

The greatest enemy we have is not of this world. It is not criminals, murderers, or terrorists. Our main enemy is Satan, and unfortunately, he is *constantly* lurking about, searching for someone's mind to invade.

This is why it is absolutely crucial to <u>always be on alert.</u> Keep your heart, mind, and soul protected by wearing the armor of God.

Stay grounded in God's truth. Do not isolate yourself. Instead, surround yourself with your brothers and sisters in Christ who will help you face the enemy head-on with great faith and strength!

Dear God,

Thank you for your protection. Make me acutely aware of Satan's schemes and lies. Do not allow anyone or anything to distract me from the subtle alarms and forewarnings. Keep my mind sharp and active, my ears perceptive, my eyes vigilant so that I can easily recognize Satan and turn from him.

December 3

By His divine power, God has given us everything we need
for living a godly life. We have received all of this
by coming to know Him, the one who called us to
Himself by means of His marvelous glory and excellence.
~2 Peter 1:3

We desire a bigger house, better job, or faster car. Our minds dwell on what the next iPhone will be and when we can hold it in our hands. We seek more and more possessions and/or relationships. We already have *everything* we need!

The Bible is our instruction manual and God provides all of our physical, emotional, and spiritual needs. No one and nothing, not even living out your heart's greatest desires and dreams, can satisfy your soul like the Lord.

Dear God,

Thank you for providing everything I need for living a godly life. Your Word instructs me about Your character and how I am to obey. Your children who are my dear brothers and sisters help me during tough times. My prayers and worship strengthen our relationship and grow my faith. I give you all the glory, honor, and praise!

December 4

*In view of all this, make every effort to respond to
God's promises. Supplement your faith with
a generous provision of moral excellence,
and moral excellence with knowledge.*
~2 Peter 1:5

We show God that we respond to His promises by
supplementing faith with moral excellence and knowledge.

Trust in the Lord's instructions and believe in His promises,
and *do what He asks* whether you understand or not. Rest
assured that when you do, blessings will follow!

Dear Father,

*Thank you for Your perfect promises. Please give me the knowledge
to understand Your direction for my life, instructions for me, and
Your will for my life. Reveal to me any area where I lack faith and
help me to let go of that worry or doubt and trust confidently in You
alone.*

December 5

*The Lord isn't really being slow about His promise, as some
people think. No, He is being patient for your sake.
He doesn't want anyone to be destroyed,
but wants everyone to repent.*
~2 Peter 3:9

Accept God's time frame with a positive attitude. Sometimes
we have absolutely no clue why we're waiting, but we must
realize that it's for good reason.

Maybe the Lord is making you wait for your spouse because
He's in the middle of crafting you into the best husband/wife
you can be. Or, He is building your future spouse into being
the best husband/wife for you. Maybe He is having you wait
for that "perfect job" because He wants you to shine His light
to those in your current workplace. Maybe you're waiting for
that financial breakthrough because He is reminding you to be
dependent on Him and building your faith!

Hurry is not His nature. Remain faithful during this time, and
wait in hopeful expectation for the blessing. Plus, long periods
of waiting only intensify your enjoyment when you receive!
Sometimes the result is not what we desire, and we must
remain thankful to God because *everything* He does in our
lives is according to His perfect will.

Dear Lord,

*Thank you for making me wait for a promise to be fulfilled. I know
You are in control and know what's best for me. Please fill me with
patience and peace as I wait. Do not let anyone or anything
influence my trust in You.*

December 6

Rather, you must grow in the grace and knowledge of our Lord and Savior Jesus Christ. All glory to Him, both now and forever! Amen!
~2 Peter 3:18

Meditate on the living Word. Fellowship with godly friends and mentors who can teach you more about the Lord.

Strengthen your personal relationship with Jesus through private time of prayer and worship.

Dear Jesus,

Thank you for your amazing grace. Please help me generously extend grace to not only my family, friends, and coworkers, but also to my enemies. Place the right people in my life who can help me grow in Your wisdom, and use me to teach others about Your glory and love.

December 7

So we are lying if we say we have fellowship with God but go on living in spiritual darkness; we aren't practicing the truth.
~1 John 1:6

The truth is that fellowship with God involves a genuine heart that seeks Him and desires to live righteously. Our sin is followed by true repentance in which we turn away from the darkness and towards Jesus, our Light.

John says here that you are lying if you decide (it's a choice) to continue living in spiritual darkness, intentionally sinning without true repentance, while telling others that you are in fellowship with God.

Dear Father,

Thank you for cleansing me of all sin. Please reveal hidden sins that I need to confess to you and repent from. I want to practice truth and live according to Your instructions. Show me how I can help others retreat from spiritual darkness and journey into Your Light.

December 8

But those who obey God's word truly show how completely
they love Him. That is how we know we are living in Him.
~1 John 2:5

Being aware of your Father and His magnificent word more
than other people or things of this world will produce
beautiful results. You will be able to show compassion,
forgive, and extend grace much easier.

Blessings come from obeying the Lord, thus obedience builds
our confidence in Him. When we witness a miracle or receive
an extraordinary blessing, our faith (trust in God) soars and
we are more confident to obey Him in the future because we
know He is faithful in all of His promises.

Dear Lord,

Thank you for Your living, active Word that nourishes my soul.
Thank you for the Holy Spirit who whispers Truth and guides me
along the path of everlasting life. Please make Your instructions for
me obvious so I can be sure that I am living in Your will. Whenever
I think I know what's best, get me back on track with a heavenly
perspective immediately – that You are in control. You are for me,
and Your plans for me are perfect.

December 9

Don't love this world nor the things it offers to you,
for when you love the world,
you don't have the love of the Father in you.
~1 John 2:15

We may start craving the lifestyle that celebrities and other wealthy people have. Television, radio, news, and advertisements often influence what we want. As we scroll through social media, we begin comparing ourselves to others, feeling inferior and depressed.

Luxurious lifestyles and material possessions are of this world. Seeking fulfillment in *things* and satisfying personal pride do not demonstrate true love to your Father. The world we live in is gradually fading away, along with *everything in it.*

Your true home is in heaven. Show God that you love Him by seeking Him first above all and doing what pleases Him.

Dear Lord,

Please take away my passion for things of this world. Instill in me a burning desire to want what You want for me. Give me the audacity to turn away anything that is not of value in Your kingdom. Give me clarity on Your instructions and fill me with absolute confidence to take action right away.

December 10

But you have received the Holy Spirit, and he lives within you, so you don't need anyone to teach you what is true. For the spirit teaches you everything you need to know, and what he teaches is true – it is not a lie. So just as he has taught you, remain in fellowship with Christ.
~1 John 2:27

God gave you His prodigious Holy Spirit as a free gift. It guides you, teaches you what's right, and advises you on decisions.

The Holy Spirit is truth and *lives inside you*, so you do not need to search the world or other people for meaning, wisdom, or fulfillment. Listen to and obey the voice within your soul.

Dear God,

Thank you for Your Holy Spirit who dwells within me. Eliminate all the noise and distractions that keep me from hearing its voice. Humble my heart and open my mind so I am able to not only feel its presence, but also respond to its promptings.

December 11

Dear children, let us not merely say that we love each other;
let us show the truth by our actions.
~1 John 3:18

Actions speak louder than words. Imagine Jesus standing next to you, watching how you treat others. Would you just walk by the woman with a baby in one arm & groceries in the other struggling to open her car door? Would you slide on past the elderly man who's clearly having trouble going up some steps? Would you yell at your spouse, children, friends, or family over the smallest things? Would you be so careless as to not help the wounded or ill when there's definitely something you can do? I don't think you would if you imagined Jesus physically being right there.

Remember, Jesus is omnipresent, so treat everyone, including strangers and adversaries, with love, for that is what He did for us.

Dear Father,

Thank you for Your profound, limitless love. Help me to love others as You love us. Show me what I can do to prove I am loving them. Remind me to always back up the words from my mouth with action, especially when it comes to love.

December 12

*But you belong to God, my dear children. You have already
won a victory over those people because the Spirit who lives
in you is greater than the spirit who lives in the world.*
~1 John 4:4

Unfortunate circumstances, unexpected problems, and
tragedies are part of life. This verse reminds us of the ultimate
victory which has already been won by God who defeated
death. His Spirit is more powerful than anything we will face
in this world.

Anxious and fearful thoughts cause us to forget that God is in
control. Remind yourself of His promises and focus on Him
during the entire battle.

Dear God,

*When I begin to fear, quickly remind me that You are with me and
the ultimate battle has already been won. Lord, help me teach others
of this incredible truth so that I may instill confidence within them.*

December 13

This is real love – not that we loved God, but that He loved us and sent His Son as a sacrifice to take away our sins.
~1 John 4:10

Perfect love is Jesus Christ because He willingly died for everyone in order to eradicate our sins and give us eternal life. Would you sacrifice your life to save sinful, unrighteous people?

Dear God,

Thank you for my salvation. Your infinite love astounds me. Please reveal to me those who need to know and experience Your love. Give me confidence to be Your mouthpiece as I share of Your incomprehensible love for him/her. Speak and work Your love through me so he/she can know and feel Your remarkable loving presence.

December 14

Since we believe human testimony, surely we can believe the
greater testimony that comes from God.
And God has testified about His son.
~1 John 5:9

The Bible is not a fictional book with made up stories or legends. The living Word shares God's testimony about His son Jesus Christ. It reveals God's character, teaches us what is pure and right, and guides us along the path of righteousness.

We are called to impact our friends and family, communities, and the world with the love and message of Jesus. We are God's ambassadors, called to build up His kingdom by reaching the lost, teaching them the Word, and bringing them to salvation. If this is all you do while here on earth, you are more wealthy than the "richest" person on the planet!

Dear Lord,

I believe that You sent Your Son Jesus to grant me eternal life by sacrificing His life on the cross. I believe the Bible is Your true and active word. Please help me confidently share the gospel with gentleness and kindness. Use me as your vessel and speak through me.

December 15

And we are confident that He hears us
whenever we ask for anything that pleases Him.
~1 John 5:14

Since we know that God hears us, we can know He will
answer.

The answer <u>may not be what you want</u> to hear, but that is
beside the point. He is Lord of all and knows what's best not
only for you, but for your loved ones, your community, and
ultimately all of mankind. He sees the completed puzzle,
whereas we only see a tiny part of one small piece of that
puzzle.

His response <u>may not be what you thought</u> it would be, but
that doesn't matter either. His ways and thoughts go above
our heads, way beyond our comprehension. His answers are
unbelievably marvelous.

His answer <u>may not come when you want</u> it to, and that is
irrelevant as well. We live in a world today where we are
continuously on the go, rushed and impatient. We grow
frustrated when our immediate access to the internet is
interrupted. We become angry when our meal takes too long
at the restaurant or we have to wait in a long line. So,
naturally, we become frustrated, weary, and/or upset when
our prayer isn't answered quickly.

God is full of patience. He waits. God already has the answer
ready at His disposal, but He waits until we are ready to
receive it and until the time is right for His plans. In His
impeccable timing, it will be given to you.

Dear God,

Thank you for hearing my cries, requests, dreams, goals, thoughts, and confessions. Although I cannot comprehend Your ways, I trust that You are in control and have not only my best interest in mind, but that of the entire world. When I am required to wait for an extended time, please keep me strong, energized, and full of faith! I know You hear me and trust that You will answer, in Your time.

December 16

*Grace, mercy, and peace, which come from God the Father
and from Jesus Christ, the Son of the Father, will continue
to be with us who live in truth and love!*
~2 John 1:3

How wonderful to know that as long as we abide in God's
love and truth, we receive His unending grace, incredible
mercy, and absolute, sound peace.

As broken and sinful people, we are in constant need of God's
grace and mercy. He freely gives it to us when we seek Him.
Halleluiah! Unforeseen circumstances, difficulties, tragedies,
and even just everyday life are enough to let anxiety and
worry take control, which is why we always need God's
peace.

Dear Lord,

*Thank you for forgiving me of my sins and blessing me with
amazing grace. Thank you for being incredibly merciful towards me
every day. Father, thank you for calming my nerves and soothing my
stressful mind.*

December 17

Love means doing what God has commanded us,
and He has commanded us to love one another,
just as you heard from the beginning.
~2 John 1:6

Above all, John wished his readers would demonstrate love towards one another and live in eternal truth. God's greatest commandment is to love one another as He loves us.

Simply look to the cross to remind yourself of God's love for you. He sent His one and only Son as a living sacrifice so that you would have the choice to choose Jesus as your savior and follow the path of life.

Dear Father,

According to your instructions and commandments, point out to me what I need to work on and help me to do so. Transform my heart and soul to be more like You.

December 18

*So we ourselves should support them so that we
can be their partners as they teach the truth.*
~3 John 1:8

When you have full-fledged support from your family, co-workers or boss, and/or friends, you feel quite confident, motivated, and positive.

Our pastors and authority figures with hearts after God not only deserve, but need our support as they teach the Truth. Partner with them as they share God's love, advise us using scripture, remind us of God's promises, and so much more.

Dear Lord,

Thank you for my pastors. Show me how I can support them through serving, giving, praying, and/or any other way they need. As your child, I know that I am called to teach the good news to others as well. I invite the Holy Spirit to speak through me as I explain the gospel.

December 19

Now all glory to God, who is able to keep you from falling
away and will bring you with great joy
into his glorious presence without a single fault.
~Jude 1:24

God is not only able to keep you from wandering away from
Him, but He is actively pursuing you because He loves you so
much.

Furthermore, He fills you with *inexplainable joy* as He brings
you into His *glorious presence!* Regardless of your past, present,
or future mistakes, failures, and sins, the Lord does this for
you! Praise the Lord your God!

Dear Father,

I praise Your holy name! Thank you for looking beyond every fault
of mine and loving me exactly as I am. Thank you for giving me free
access to your glorious presence at all times.

December 20

Do not be afraid of what you are about to suffer.
The devil will throw some of you into prison to test you.
You will suffer for 10 days. But if you remain faithful even
when facing death, I'll give you the crown of life.
~Revelation 2:10

View disaster, sorrow, or pain as a rich growing opportunity.
Your Teacher is right at your side during that hardship. Jesus
knows your situation and will meet you right where you are.

God is strengthening you, teaching you a valuable lesson,
bringing you closer to Him, and/or glorifying His name by
showing others how you persevere by trusting in Him. Thank
God for all trials and suffering so they lose power to drag you
down. See them as temporary situations that are producing
God's glory!

Offer your burdens, pain, worries, and fears to God! He will
dive down into the depths and pull you out of the dark
waters. God breaks chains. *Joy will emerge through your*
thankfulness and praise!

Dear Lord,

Thank you for bearing my burdens and carrying my worries. I
believe with my whole heart that You will use my suffering for good
in Your kingdom. Please help me to remain focused on You and to
not lose faith during this challenging time. Set me free from the
shackles of fear and worry. Provide relief from the strenuous tasks
ahead. Give me unlimited endurance and strength to push on.

December 21

I know all the things you do, and I have opened a door for you
that no one can close. You have little strength,
yet you obeyed my word and did not deny me.
~Revelation 3:8

Your heavenly Father knows your every thought before you even think it. He knows every lie you've told. He is aware of all your sins. Even though it can be very hard to confess, repent and turn back to God. Never deny who He is – your faithful Father who loves you unconditionally and forgives you always.

What God opens no one can close, and what He closes no one can open. Even if you're powerless and exhausted, obey the Lord while trusting that He has a plan and purpose for you. He will open that door to relief, to joy, and to the miracle you are yearning for!

Dear God,

Thank you for being in total control. Because You are a sovereign, just, and good Lord above all, I trust in both the doors you open and the ones you close. Give me a heavenly perspective and a thankful attitude when a door I want to enter is blocked by Your hand as well as when a door I am hesitant to walk through is wide open by You.

December 22

I correct and discipline everyone I love.
So be diligent and turn from your indifference.
~Revelation 3:19

God doesn't punish out of anger or hatred. He does so out of love, teaching us grace, strengthening us spiritually, and building our patience.

He does not need to explain himself, and you don't need to have all the details upfront to obey. To be diligent means to persevere and *work hard*, so here, we are instructed to conscientiously turn away from our negligence. Accept the Lord's correction and learn from it.

Dear Lord,

Thank you for Your discipline. I know that You are purifying my heart and enhancing my character. You are teaching me what You want me to learn. Father, give me a teachable spirit and a thankful attitude for when correction comes my way from You as well as from others.

December 23

Look! I stand at the door and knock.
If you hear my voice and open the door, I will come in,
and we will share a meal together as friends.
~Revelation 3:20

We choose to invite God into our hearts or not. He never forces us to do anything. He speaks to us, waiting ever so patiently for our response, yearning for us to reconnect with Him.

If you invite God into to your heart and surrender to His ways, then you will certainly experience His presence. Stay in God's house, continue reading the Bible, and surround yourself with others who love the Lord.

Dear God,

Thank you for having so much compassion for me and for never giving up on me. Drown out the noise of the world so I can hear your knock, shield my eyes from sin and temptation, and destroy Satan's lies the instant they come to mind. I invite You into my heart today and forever, for You are my Lord and Savior.

December 24

*You are worthy, O Lord our God, to receive glory and honor
and power. For you created all things, and they exist
because You created what You pleased.*
~Revelation 4:11

There would be absolutely nothing without our supreme God!
He deserves **all** glory, honor, praise, and worship not just
today, but forever; not just when life is going well for you, but
in times of distress and misery as well.

All that we are, everything we have, and all that is of this
world is truly from God Almighty. God's supremacy and
abilities are beyond comprehension. Ponder in His
astonishing power and glory.

Dear God,

*Thank you for the masterpieces in nature that You've created. Thank
you for the divine situations You placed me in. Your strong hand
can make the impossible possible in an instant if that is Your will.
Your brilliant glory illuminates the darkest of places. I give You all
the honor and praise today and forever!*

December 25

This means that God's holy people must endure persecution
patiently, obeying His commands
and maintaining their faith in Jesus.
~Revelation 14:12

If you are being mistreated for any reason, remain calm and patient. Accept the situation, praying to the Lord to reveal what His purpose is. Rejoice in what God is doing even though it's beyond your understanding.

God already has it all planned out. Do not worry. Don't let go of your faith!

Dear Lord,

Please fix my composure to maintain self-control and poise as I endure maltreatment and oppression. Give me extra patience during this time. Please make me especially kind before my enemies. Do not let anyone or anything weaken my faith in You.

December 26

And they were singing the song of Moses, "Great and marvelous are your works, O Lord God, the Almighty. Just and true are your ways, O King of the nations."
~Revelation 15:3

With every step you take, trust the mighty King wholeheartedly. Sing praises to Him joyfully! Declare thanksgiving to Him.

Follow where God leads without worrying how the situation or you yourself will turn out and without analyzing the process or result. Concentrate on taking one step at a time *with Him.*

Dear Father,

Thank you for being a fair and compassionate King. Teach me your ways and help me to apply Your instructions. I worship You for Your astounding ways and perfect justice.

December 27

Let us be glad and rejoice, and let us give honor to Him.
For the time has come for the wedding feast of the Lamb,
and His bride has prepared herself.
~Revelation 19:7

The church, Jesus' bride, is to be faithful to God the Father. Those who trust in Jesus as their personal savior make up the church. The church is not merely a building. Christ's church is made up of the body of believers. He calls us to be disciples, teaching the good news.

When the wedding feast of the Lamb comes, we will feel elated beyond measure because Jesus blesses everyone invited to that supper.

Dear God,

Thank you for your faithfulness. I pray that everyone who believes in you as their Lord realizes that church is not just a building, but it is themselves who make up a body for Your kingdom. Unite us together in love and peace.

December 28

I heard a loud shout from the throne, saying,
"Look, God's home is now among his people! He will live
with them, and they will be His people.
God Himself will be with them."
~Revelation 21:3

Praise God! Just relax.

We always *want to be sure* of things. We want to know without any doubt that the new refrigerator will function as the company says, be certain that our food will be prepared how we ask, be sure that our paycheck is deposited into our bank account, and be sure that our best friend will be there when we need him/her.

The only clear, unquestionable thing is that there is no certainty, except for the fact that you are God's child and His spirit lives within you. You can be 100% certain that Jesus Christ died on the cross for your salvation and that He will rescue you in times of trouble! You can also be absolutely sure that God is always with You and His plans are to prosper not harm you.

God's will be done. Trust Him. Breathe.

Dear God,

Thank you for your tender Spirit who guides me and for Your Son Jesus. Thank you for the amazing plans You have for my life. Reveal these plans to me and show me the path You want me to take because I only desire to be in Your will. I trust You Lord.

December 29

He will wipe every tear from their eyes, and there will be
no more death or sorrow or crying or pain.
All these things are gone forever.
~Revelation 21:4

Depression, hopelessness, panic, and terror will be
immediately replaced with happiness, hope, and confidence
when you are with Jesus in heaven. There will be no more
horror, evil acts, or anguish!

Our darkest times are opportunities for Jesus to shine brightly.
He will lead the way for us, while also using our trials to show
others His glorious light. With Him, we can rise out of ashes.

Dear God,

Thank you for accepting me into Your kingdom in heaven. I am
forever grateful. Give me the courage to boldly say, "I will not fear"
to whatever comes my way.

December 30

And He also said, "It is finished. I am the Alpha and the Omega – the Beginning and the End. To all who are thirsty I will give freely from the springs of the water of life."
~Revelation 21:6

We don't have to pay or barter to receive love, grace, mercy, or forgiveness from God. All we need to do is accept Jesus as our Savior, repent of our sins, declare that the Lord is our God, and do our very best to walk on His righteous path. Not only will he give us what we need, but he does so *freely* without asking for anything in return. In addition, God blesses those who trust in Him, wait upon Him, and have faith in Him.

Jesus suffered the worst possible death, sacrificing his life so we all can have salvation and live in heaven for eternity, even though he knew not everyone would accept Him into their hearts.

Dear Jesus,

You are my Savior! Thank you for giving up your life so that I am cleansed from all sin. Thank you for the free invitation to live in heaven for eternity! Whenever I need anything, I will seek you because You are the only One who can fully satisfy my every need.

December 31

And there will be no night there – no need for lamps or sun –
for the Lord God will shine on them.
And they will reign forever and ever.
~Revelation 22:5

You may feel terribly distant from God, but that's just a feeling, not reality. God is always right at your side. He is a faithful, compassionate Father.

We are lost, confused, and/or frightened in darkness, both literally and figuratively. God's radiant light expels all darkness, so do not fear.

Dear Lord,

Thank you for continuously shining Your light to keep me from being stuck in darkness. I choose to follow Your path of righteousness and obey Your instructions. Father, give me wisdom and discernment as I navigate through life. Reveal Your will to me. Keep my faith in You strong and steady. Thank you for being so incredibly compassionate to me and completely faithful in all of Your promises. I trust in You, Your ways, and Your timing.

<u>Thank You</u>

Billy, my wonderful husband: Thank you for loving me unconditionally, supporting my goals and dreams, always making me laugh, and encouraging me daily. Thank you for working so hard to provide for our family. I love you with all my heart!

Mom and Dad: Thank you for raising me in a safe, nurturing, joyful home. Thank you for your endless love and support

C.J. and Tim: Thank you for always looking out for me! I am so blessed to call you my brothers.

To the rest of my family: Thank you for modeling forgiveness, grace, kindness, compassion, and love! Thank you for uplifting me and praying for me over the years.

To all of my friends & my church family: Thank you for simply being my friend and helping whenever I'm in need.

I know without a doubt that God placed every single one of you in my life for His purpose. <u>You each have a special place in my heart.</u>

To all of my readers: Thank you for taking time to read *Rest in God's Word*. I pray it provides comfort, instills peace within your soul, and gives you the encouragement you need. I pray that reading it helps connect you with the Lord more and that you are able to discern what His will is for your life.

May God bless each of you always!

About the Author

Kelly grew up in Ft. Wayne, Indiana with her loving parents, older brother C.J., younger brother Tim, and many pets throughout her childhood. She thanks God daily for giving her parents who raised their children to know about Jesus. Both her mother and father modeled what it meant to be the hands and feet of Jesus through generously tithing to church and giving to those in need. They served at church, at school, and in their community. Her parents also modeled extending forgiveness, having grace, being compassionate, and above all, loving everyone.

Growing up in a safe and nurturing home with Jesus at the center is certainly one of the biggest blessings Kelly praises God for. Her parents have always been incredibly supportive, encouraging, and helpful to Kelly as a child, teenager, and to this day as an adult. She is forever grateful to the Lord for them.

Kelly's older brother C.J. passed away at the young age of 26 in January of 2014. This was the saddest time of her life, but she kept her eyes on Jesus, trusting Him to provide comfort and peace. She stayed in connection with Him through prayer and remained on His path, which enabled her to see how He was working the tragedy into good. Kelly's favorite verse has always been Romans 8:28, which was especially helpful during this time.

Kelly and her younger brother Tim were very close growing up. They would always play games indoors and out, have "sleep overs" in each other's rooms, and make hilarious home videos together. They spent much less time together as teenagers because of work, different friends, and different interests. Now as adults, although they live in separate states, they are very close again. Kelly feels beyond blessed to have an amazing younger brother.

Kelly has enjoyed writing ever since she could pick up a pencil and form her first letters! It didn't matter whether she was assigned a narrative, opinion piece, poem, research paper, or other writing task in school. She would joyfully grab a pencil and begin. In first grade, she got her first journal and wrote "Dear Journal" nearly every day.

She fell in love with poetry in elementary school. A natural writer, Kelly is humbled to have published her first book, a devotional called *Rest in God's Word*. She has other pieces that she's currently working on and says that she will publish whichever one(s) God lays on her heart to do so.

The Lord instilled a profound love for animals within Kelly's soul from the moment she was born. She loves them all, and is always eager to educate others on pet care, health, and behavior. She grew up with dogs and cats, as well as a variety of other pets including rabbits, guinea pigs, hamsters, lizards, and birds. She worked at a pet store for throughout high school and college. Going to work there filled her heart with pure joy as she helped customers with their pets and pet needs.

After graduating from Indiana University in 2012 with her bachelor's in elementary education, she moved to Florida to leave the cold northern winters for good! She began her teaching career that fall. Since then, she has taught everything from kindergarten through seventh grade in both public and private Christian schools. From working at pet stores, zoos, and veterinary offices during the summer months, Kelly always found a way to pursue her deep love for animals and passion for customer service. In 2017, she opened an LLC business for pet sitting and dog training. Her kindness, trustworthiness, knowledge, and experience give owners complete peace of mind when they leave their pets in her care. Her years of dog training experience and communication skills are what make her successful in dog training.

The greatest desire of Kelly's heart has always been to be a wife and a mother. After years and years of praying, waiting, and trusting the Lord, He introduced Billy to her in September 2020 (she was 31). God's hand is clearly all over their journeys and story, which is a whole other book that will be written one day. Billy proposed 6 months later, and they both couldn't be happier that the Lord's promise and blessing to give them a spouse finally came! Although Kelly closed her pet sitting and dog training business that March (2021) due to entering a new season of wedding planning and marrying her best friend, she continues caring for others' pets and training dogs to this day when she has free time.

Kelly and her husband started their own drywall company, *Reliford Drywall LLC*, in August 2021. They give all glory to God because He clearly planned this out long ago! The Lord paired Billy's gifts of working with his hands, his knowledge and experience with drywall and construction, and his strong communication skills with Kelly's strengths of organization, budgeting and dealing with finances, computer skills, and excellent customer service. They absolutely love working <u>together</u> and helping people in need. They place God first and have a motto of *"Service from the Heart."*

Both Kelly and Billy are dedicated to following wherever the Lord leads because they know His ways are perfect. They trust in His will and timing. They both pray that others see Jesus' light through them. They pray everyone develops a personal relationship Jesus Christ and accepts Him as their personal savior.

Made in the USA
Columbia, SC
24 April 2023

15404655R00228